BECAUSE OF C

A
PERSONAL PORTFOLIO
OF
YULETIDE REMEMBRANCES

by
Marcus Bach

Photographs by Lorena Bach

LITTLE BOOKS FOR LIFELONG LEARNING

FELLOWSHIP FOR SPIRITUAL UNDERSTANDING
Palos Verdes Estates
California

LITTLE BOOKS FOR LIFELONG LEARNING
FELLOWSHIP FOR SPIRITUAL UNDERSTANDING
P.O. Box 816, Palos Verdes Estates
California 90274

Printed in the United States of America.

ISBN 0-940581-00-0

Dedicated to all who treat the Christmastide
with love and peace.

Books by Marcus Bach

THE POWER OF PERCEPTION
THE WORLD OF SERENDIPITY
THE WILL TO BELIEVE
THE POWER OF TOTAL LIVING
MAJOR RELIGIONS OF THE WORLD
I, MONTY
QUESTIONS ON THE QUEST
THE UNITY WAY
LET LIFE BE LIKE THIS
GOD AND THE SOVIETS
MAKE IT AN ADVENTURE
WHAT'S RIGHT WITH THE WORLD

BECAUSE OF CHRISTMAS

Contents

1   BECAUSE OF CHRISTMAS

2   MEMORY, MEANING, AND MIRACLE

3   MONSIEUR MINUIT   *A Vignette*

4   NOSTALGIA

5   CREATIVITY

6   LOS PASTORES   *A Drama*

7   SOMEWHERE, SOMEHOW, SOMETIME

8   WHAT'S NEW ABOUT CHRISTMAS

9   WHEN ADONAIAH OAKIE
        SAW THE STAR   *A Parable*

10 OF MOTHER AND CHILD

11 CHRISTMAS IN OTHER LANDS

12 OF CHRISTMAS TIME AND TIDE   *A Fantasy*

Chapter One

Because of Christmas

BECAUSE OF CHRISTMAS

1.

The Setting

Because of Christmas something wonderful happens to the world. Most of us have known this from childhood and have believed it ever since we saw our first string of colored lights or heard the sound of carols on a wintry night. Something told us that *God is real and life is good.*

Remembering this, let's take another look at the crowds, the traffic, the jam-packed malls, the freeways, the fanfare of it all, and see the commonly unseen: *Within the Christmas of the American way lies the Christmas of the American heart.*

Because of Christmas we know that the heart of America, despite all appearances and imperfections, is reflective and sincere. It remembers not only friends and fellow-workers, it reaches out to help the needy, the homeless, the unknown. It is as perfect as you and I, and at this time of year it renders service, as we all do to some degree, without thought of recognition or reward.

Because of Christmas we feel the fellowship of kindred spirits, of something deeper than the gift that's given, and we know instinctively that beyond the frenzy of it all, a hopeful quiet lies ahead, gift-wrapped in a day of peace when the world is strangely still and we are *conscious of our deepest self.*

Someday a special genius will come along with a plan, a system, and a technique for extending the supernormal magic of the *day* into weeks and months and eventually into a year, bridging the gap from Christmas to Christmas until we say, "Why didn't someone think of this long ago?"

The truth is, Someone did, but apparently He made it too simple. From the humble setting of a manger He merely asked us to remember that *God is real and life is good.*

2.

Down Under

During one Advent season my wife, Lorena, and I were on a writing-photographic assignment "down-under," in the Commonwealths of Australia, Tasmania, and New Zealand.

It was spring as far as nature was concerned, but Christmas was in the air. Something magical was happening around us, and something mystical was happening within us as well. When talking with friends we usually found ourselves saying, "Christmas is truly universal. Christian and non-Christian feel its spell. There is something supernatural about it. It crosses international boundaries and hemispheric lines. It is unstopped by borders, cultures, or customs. It creates its own consciousness and charts its own course."

Because of Christmas we had a will to believe in a Power higher and greater than ourselves. Christmas made us more responsive, intimate, confident, as if this Higher Power could be depended upon, as if God, who had often seemed far afield throughout the year, was now back in His heaven and all was once more right with the world. Christmas engendered trust. The mystical star was shining. The touch of a miraculous birth was all around us.

Even when I picked up the evening paper and realized that nothing much had changed in the world, things had changed in me because of Christmas. It was winter somewhere, but it was also spring. Just now there were no "foreign" countries, no strangers, no terrestrial limits, no religious, cultural or economic lines, no north or south, east or west — there was only Christmas, and every village and every home was Bethlehem of old.

3.

Discovering the Oneness

It was at such a moment, in such a mood, that I met a stranger in the quiet surroundings of the magnificent city library in Sydney. I was looking for material on the Australian aborigines, and here was a friendly, bearded young man sitting across from me. At one point, as we both happened to look up from our reading, our eyes met. He smiled when he took notice of the pile of reference books in which I had been absorbed for the past hour.

I went back to my reading. He got up and walked away. I saw him climb the two flights of stairs into the huge gallery where thousands of colorful volumes were catalogued in open stacks. In a a few moments he returned, bringing with him a lovely publication: *We the Aborigines* by Douglas Lockwood. Without a word he opened the book to a certain page, laid it before me on the table, and quietly walked away.

The chapter was titled, "Baby Matthew", a story of the Wailbri aboriginal tribe. It began with a poem:

"One night beside a campfire's glow,
I heard a Songman chanting low
A song of life. And overhead
The stars gleamed bright, and this he said:

"Life is a day, and as the dawn
Comes from the earth, a child is born
Grim night departs, dawn lights the sky,
And with it comes the infant's cry.

"The earth-ones give
The wise ones know,
The tribes shall live
As children grow.

"The sun comes up, so grows the child,
Meekly at first, then strong and wild,
Noisy as birds that sweep and cry
That strong ones live as weak ones die.

"Thus children play
for elders know
Strength comes to those
Who thrive and grow.

"The day grows bright, the sun is strong,
So grows the youngster sleek and strong,
And as a tree spreads strong with shade,
The Elders meet and a man is made.

"The totems give
The Elders know
The tribe shall live
As children grow."

In the silence of the library, where I was almost alone now, I read on:

"My Mummy loves me just as much as any white mother, perhaps more. She is not obligated to waste a lot of mush love on my Daddy, and is thus able to give it all to me."

"We have only one wind level, one fire, and one blanket each. We huddle together to keep warm in winter. Mum often has to get up to stoke the fire, and it is then that I see her crawl into my Dad's blanket.

"I hope you don't think I was conceived and born as the result of sexual intercourse. Some of the sophisticated natives say that a man can give a woman a child in this way. But we know better than that. My Mum and Dad know that I was created by a spirit entering her body.

"You laugh? Nonsense, you say? Yet I heard you say you were a Christian. If that is so, you must believe in a virgin birth. Then why laugh at us if we think babies are formed by spirit children who pass into the mother while she sleeps?

"By the way, my name is Matthew. We live two hundred miles northwest of Alice Springs on the fringe of the Great Sandy Desert."

I closed my eyes. Because of Christmas, thoughts rushed through my mind and words kept coming back to me:

> "The earth-ones give,
> The wise ones know,
> The tribe shall live
> As children grow."

Did I say that every village and every home is Bethlehem? I should have said, "Every heart." For far across the reaches of mankind, from aboriginal to the most sophisticated son of man, the star was shining and there were signs of the miracle of Christmas.

Something was telling me loud and clear that *God is real and life is good.* But, then, that was something I had known from childhood and had believed in ever since I saw my first string of colored lights and heard the sound of carols on a winter's night.

4.

Hometown

I remember Christmas in a little Wisconsin town where I lived as a boy. It was an American Christmas, but it was also German and Swiss in keeping with the customs of my parents who came from these countries. Through their traditional observances I was introduced to life in the very heart of continental Europe.

Though I had never been away from home, I smelled the Christmas cooking in Lucerne and Stuttgart. I can smell it now, the cinnamon cakes, the anise cookies, the pear bread, the marzipan. I can feel the warmth of the open oven when my mother took the *Voecke* from the stove. Christmas customs, from the lighting of the *Advent Kranz* to the songs and prayers and the making of the creche were Swiss-German, but they were also American. Because of the freedom which permitted us to enjoy these bits of culture from the shores of other lands, we loved America more, and we knew that just across the river from our town were Poles, Hungarians, and

Irish, keeping Christmas according to the countries of their birth.

None of this has been lost. The pattern of life is still the same, and if ever you feel that some of the charm is gone, if you feel your Christmas has grown small and is no longer the same, it may be that *you* have changed. If so, it is you who can, if you will, recapture the spirit of the days when you used to say, "Let life be like this!"

Recapture the Christmas spirit by way of appreciation. By gratitude. By selflessness. By honesty in your sense of values, by facing yourself squarely. By taking an honest look at the image you have built, which may or may not be your real image. Perhaps simply by a recall of your youth or counting your blessings or by the challenge of the Yuletide saying that,

"Those who find Christmas in their hearts,
Find Christmas everywhere."

5.

A World Without Christmas

Who can imagine an old year ending or a new year being born without the Christmas spirit locking up the flight of time and releasing it anew?

That's how it is with life, with those moments of special joy, the wonderful "highs of consciousness," the overtones of heightened spiritual awareness. *Make the most of them, and let them always be special points of growth!*

Christmas! At least once in the round of seasons and the familiar seasonal cycle, we catch the magic of a deepened insight into the stuff of life and find a certain miracle within ourselves. Once a year we realize we are the same persons we always were, but we are different. Strangers, friends, relatives, the boss, all the same, but at Christmas all are different. Neighborhoods, town and country, all the same, all different. Christmas Eve, a night like any other night, but *different.* All of which is part of the miracle.

Life does have its miracles, and Christmas is proof of it.

They say that miracles are not really miracles, they are demonstrations of a law by those who know the working of the law.

Well and good. So let's learn the miracle of knowing the law. *Every breakthrough into a higher wave length of being is such a time and Christmas, fleeting though it may be, is a time that proves the law that "As a man thinketh in his heart, so is he."*

I remember snow on Christmas Eve. It was different from snow at other times. Softer. Gentler. More fun. There was a special stillness about it. There was a mood about it. A kind of reverence. I was seeing it through the eyes of youth, and one of the miracles of Christmas is that we can work the miracle of retrospection.

Now I live where it never snows, but the enchantment of the nights before Christmas years ago is there just the same. The hush, the feeling, the spirit are there. They are mine. They are yours. Recall can be therapeutic. It depends upon the "recaller." Wherever you are on *this* Christmas Eve, you are endowed, if you wish, with the art of imagery.

I happen to be in a Southern California urban setting, thrilling, different, but reminiscent. What in the world has happened? What is this metamorphosis that silences traffic, gift-wraps the homes, and touches the impersonal surroundings with a special spell? Those stars, were they always so bright? The aura of the city, was it always so soft, so mystical on other nights? I remember snow falling among the street lights in a one-horse town on Christmas Eve.

What it is trying to tell us, of course, is that in our recall we should learn to extend the spirit beyond this night, beyond Christmas, beyond the dawning of another year.

Some motivators have tried to give us techniques on how this might be done. I, too, have a "how to" in the matter.

It concerns a monk I met in Sojiji Temple in Tokyo, Japan. I sat with him during the periods of early morning meditation, motionless, contemplative, still.

I was much impressed with him during his work-a-day world, at the way he conducted himself, his sense of calm tranquility and integrated self.

I asked him, "How do you get this way?"

He said, "I never leave my place of meditation."

The answer stayed with me. I have thought about it a great deal. I have written about it.

I remember it now at Christmas, for the way to prolong the spirit of this day is never to leave it. Then it will never leave you.

How do we do it? We do it! We do it by remembering, by being grateful, by being sensitive, aware, thoughtful, selfless, strong in the spirit of Him whom the day honors and Who has honored us. A world without Christmas? Unthinkable!

6.

Once Upon a Poem

> "Judean hills are holy,
> Judean hills are fair,
> But one can find the footprints
> Of Jesus everywhere.
>
> "One finds them in the silence
> Beneath the swinging sky
> Where shepherds watched in wonder
> White planets wheeling by.
>
> "His trails are on the hillsides
> And down the dales and deeps,
> He walks the high horizons
> Where vesper silence sleeps.

"He haunts the lowly hillsides
Where human hopes have trod.
The Via Dolorosa
Up to the heart of God.

"Judean hills are holy,
Judean fields are fair,
But one can find the footprints
Of Jesus everywhere."

— William Stidger

I memorized and never forgot the lines after hearing and getting to know the author, "Big Bill" Stidger, Methodist minister, pastor of a prestigious church in Kansas City. "Big Bill" was a hard-hitting preacher. He once invited the "infidel" Sinclair Lewis to speak in his pulpit during the Advent season. Lewis brazenly defied God by saying, "If You exist, I'll give you five minutes to strike me dead!" We waited entranced as the moments ticked off. We had mingled feelings when Lewis snapped shut the cover of his gold and shining watch and challenged us with, "What do you have to say to that? Is there a God? If there is, why doesn't He accept my challenge?"

Later Stidger said, "God did strike him dead, but Lewis doesn't know it as yet!"

"Big Bill", a child at heart, revealed his philosphy best at Christmastime when he wrote "Judean Hills".

7.

And on a City Street

I come home from a Christmas Eve church service in the booming West Coast city where I live, and I walk my Schnauzer dog. He's a patient fellow. Since early evening he has been lying near the packages in the living room, among the boxes and bows, thoughtfully wondering why this night is different, and maybe knowing, who knows? It is said by some that on Christmas Eve the cattle are lowing and animals hold their secret conversations. So why not my Schnauzer dog?

I walk him around old familiar streets. He sniffs and waggles as if life's greatest moment is just to be where he is and just to be with me.

I see the shadow of a man coming toward me out of the dark. He is not walking a dog. He is just walking. A yard light atop a Santa Claus gives me a silhouette of this stranger. He is slightly bearded, thirty perhaps, and has a small child, a girl, by the hand.

They catch sight of my dog and me and together greet us with, "Merry Christmas!" My greeting is as spontaneous as theirs, "Merry Christmas to you!"

Something in the air brings us together as if we're old friends, and the girl bends down to fondle the dog. I am amazed to learn they live only five doors from us and that we have passed many times on other nights without speaking.

After a happy talk we part as we met. "Merry Christmas" is both greeting and farewell. I hear the young girl "ohing" and "ahing" about the strings of colored lights that decorate the houses and the full-sized cut-out Santa with the light on top of his head, and I hear her say, "Why don't we always have lights like this, Daddy? Why only at Christmas?"

The obvious question is: Do we make Christmas or does Christmas make us? The obvious answer: *It is reciprocal.* We make it. It makes us. It is an event in history and a phenomenon in time. It is an episode in us.

The Spirit of Christmas is the Spirit of life, newly born, newly recognized, miraculous according to a law of love and life.

Hang up a special star! Unwrap your spiritual gifts! Kneel down and give thanks! Sing a new song! It's Christmas!

The miracle is that something has happened — not out there somewhere — but to us. To you and me. The greatness of Christmas is that it inspires us to look at life through a shepherd's eyes or a Wise Man's knowing.

At least once a year we catch the vision of a deepened insight and are persuaded that most of the world's people feel the same responses, the same wish to be as friendly and free and as happy as we. For this brief moment of spiritual oneness we stand together in consciousness realizing that even though our places in life may be different, they are alike, and though our customs and our cultures seem strangely far apart — *because of Christmas, they are one.*

Chapter Two

Memory, Meaning, and Miracle

MEMORY, MEANING,
AND MIRACLE

Memory

In the drama called *Christmas* played on the stage of your life and mine, the role of MEMORY is that of a prompter in the wings, cueing us in on scenes and lines that reach back through the years.

True, there may be some Christmases you want to forget, as a student reminded me long ago, referring to his traumatic visions of a Christmas as a POW in a war he could not seem to forget. But gradually he found his feeling absolved by recalling Christmases he had not fully appreciated during his pre-war years. Counting our blessings and recalling our "good" are Christmas impulses persuading us to sort through memory's bank for treasures we may have overlooked at other times of searching.

One interesting phase about memory's input for our Christmas season is its skill in creating the phenomenon of *de-ja vu,* the seeming replay of bygone scenes. With memory's magic touch, that which would otherwise seem silly becomes quite sacred.

For example, when now as a grown-up, I carry a five-foot Christmas tree from a busy Los Angeles fenced-in lot, after having shelled out $50 plus tax and manipulated the tree atop my car with the hope that all I am doing is within the law and that traffic will not be too heavy, I recall how my father and I used to go into the Wisconsin hills when I was knee-high to Santa Claus, and how we selected a lovely evergreen from our town's Christmas forest, all legally and without charge. Memory brings back the scene, the sounds, the scent of the needles — and not of that one Christmas only, but a chain of recollections of many Yuletide festivals along the way, reminding me of how I had to climb a ladder to clamp the angel on the tip of the tree as if I were God putting Gabriel where he belonged — memory whispering things to me in a prompter's voice.

But why go into that, since you have your memories, too, in your own memory bank: secrets, confidences, classified information and your own most private periods of *de-ja* vu. As you look back at the subject of Christmas trees, what does memory share with you?

It tells me that in the enchanted days of early boyhood I was convinced that Christmas was primarily for children.

Everything that happened during the days before the 25th, from mother's *bakerei* to the transformation of the town and its churches, the emphasis was on youth. In carols and Yuletide parties, in the merchandising on Main Street and in the fairylands of toys, it was a children's festival. The object was to answer the question, "What would you like for Christmas?" What were some of your customary requests? How did they change through your teenage years and on into early adulthood? Can you see any relevant connection between your Christmas wishes and your character development as you appraise it now?

While I was in my pre-teen years, I wanted toy soldiers and usually found them, as requested, in orderly regiments under the tree. My older brother put in a bid for a BB gun, but Santa, by the grace of God, brought him a camera with which to do his shooting.

For in those days, memory reminds me, the giving and receiving of gifts was the theme for the season. But while we were always excited and secretive about what we gave to Mother and Dad, Christmas was not without a deeper spiritual overtone, an emphasis on the coming of the "Bethlehem Child."

The songs we learned were filled with adoration on the "Christ Child" theme. "Away in a manger, no crib for a bed," "When Mary birthed Jesus 'twas in a cow's stall," "What Child is this who, laid to rest, on Mary's lap is sleeping?," "Silent night, holy night, all is calm, all is bright," "Oh, little town of Bethlehem, how still we see thee lie!" or one of the many spirituals, such as:

"Oh, Mary, what you gonna name
That pretty little baby?
Glory, glory, glory
To the newborn King!
Some will call Him one thing,
But I think I'll call him Jesus!
Glory, glory, glory,
To the newborn King!
Some will call Him one thing,
But I think I'll say Emmanuel!
Glory, glory, glory
To the newborn King!"

The manger scene, the creches, the story of the Babe wrapped in swaddling clothes, Who was honored alike by shepherds in the field and by Wise Men from the East, all these focused on the infant Jesus, himself a gift, so I was taught, to save the world and me.

All of which was enough to persuade me, without being told, to put away the soldiers and modify the thought that armies, even Christian armies, *"marching as to war,"* were hardly in the spirit of the Prince of Peace.

Memory reminds me that it was during these early, formative years that a certain tenderness about human relations took form in me. If these early convictions had any validity, they ultimately grew into a feeling about the oneness of all humankind. That not all people were *Christians* and that some might scoff at Christmas made no difference.

Memory knew better, it has its own inner knowing. It knew that during the Christmas period all people were lifted up, drawn together, united by a secret spell that made us *all* God's children at heart and *all* God's people in mind. Christmas, as far as I was concerned, was one of the greatest ideas in the world, but it needed time to catch on.

So memory said to me.

And how did it speak to you along *your* Christmas way?

2.

Meaning

The second "M", applying to the MEANING of Christmas, suggests that we ask ourselves how our views about the day and the season have changed since our fledgling years?

Somewhere along the way to adulthood we were alerted to the need for recognizing Jesus the Child as something more than just "kid's stuff." We were also reminded that in order to understand the theological implications of the plan of salvation, we would need to put aside childish things. That admonition was, in many cases, unfortunate. It may be okay to put away childish toys, but let's be wary of putting away childlike dreams, and realities which we bring with us from our unborn past.

The intercession of Christ and the edgy balance between heaven and hell were, understandably, serious business, though the precise meaning of "being saved" and the method of saving were not always clear to us who were not theologically minded. In my case, the going was tough, caught as I often was between Protestant and Catholic dialectics, and equally influenced by a humanistic father and a deeply committed, dogmatically informed mother.

In my heart, as long as I can remember, the free and open quest for "truth" was always a "first priority." Nor was it easy for me to put away "childish things" in the sense of responses to the *Christmas* Jesus, responses which had been inspirationally induced and never upset by intellectual challenges.

I lived most comfortably with the boy Jesus of Nazareth who in Joseph's carpenter shop, according to legend, quietly carved wooden birds out of scraps of cast-off lumber, tossed them into the air and watched them as they came to life and flew away. How like God that really was! The meaning was perfectly clear, and why couldn't the theologians let it go at that? God was beyond our grasp, but not beyond our reach. If He could make a world like Planet Earth, spinning in space without us earthlings falling off, surely He could make wooden birds fly when His chosen Son did the carving. That was the meaning and, because of Christmas, it was clear.

The theologians couldn't let it go at that because this kind of meaning was too naive for their grown up exegetical domain of *truth*. It was valid only up to a certain point. There was a world out there that needed sterner stuff and not only the romance and legends about love, life, and learning, but some greater reason for Christ's coming!

The reason was what the early church fathers called "soteriology," spiritual salvation. While the method by which salvation is achieved differed according to different churches, it linked Christmas inextricably with Easter, and the Child Jesus with the Risen Christ. The cradle and the cross became inseparable and this, according to prophecy, was what God had always had in mind.

Who was I to go against the prophets? In fact, the birth and the resurrection persuaded me that somewhere in this reasoning was a hidden meaning of what Christianity was all about. What was that hidden meaning? "Peace on Earth and Spiritual Understanding to all people of Goodwill, no matter what their color, creed, or culture chanced to be."

And whenever Christmas came, with its *Joy to the World*, its *We Three Kings of Orient Are*, its *God Rest You Merry, Gentlemen*, and Christmas lights and the Christmas spirit, I was back again in Bethlehem.

Following the Star, I was with Him when he outwitted the theologians in the temple and during His "hidden years" when He prepared Himself for His ministry. At Christmas in the midst of the joy and emulation, we often felt His aloneness, His forgiveness, and His love. Who could help but be drawn to Him or try, if one possibly could, to live by the principles He tried so hard to prove!

Another Meaning

A breakthough into a new MEANING about Christmas came during a Yuletide period when Lorena and I spent the holiday in Williamsburg, Virginia. The gift we gave ourselves was a painting by Quaker preacher-artist Edward Hicks: *The Peaceable Kingdom.*

With the 17-1/2″ x 23-1/2″ oil on canvas painting came a resume of the life of Edward Hicks (1780-1849). A contemporary of Frances Scott Key of *The Star-Spangled Banner* fame, Hicks was less interested in "bombs bursting in air" than he was in a new and daring concept. His painting told the story of human beings striving not only for peace among themselves, as in the "Holy Experiment" of William Penn (1644-1718), but also in living at peace with the animal kingdom, all being part of God's creation!

So here we had Penn with the signers of his Peace Treaty, together with a graphic sketch of Isaiah's prophecy, "The wolf shall dwell with the lamb, and the leopard shall lie down with the kid...and a little child shall lead them." (Isaiah 11:6) The "child" among the peaceable stylized animals was definitely the manger Child with cherubs also in the act, all adding up to a millenialistic, utopian dream of things to come.

The meaning was instantly clear: Not only had a Mediator come to save us from our sins and to pay for sins we had reneged on paying, not only was His mission to assure us of a life in a world beyond, but He had also come with the imperishable dream that all of God's children could have a Kingdom of Heaven here on earth, not only on a people-to-people basis, but including a fellowship with all living things! It was something to think about and enough to give Christmas a challenging new dimension.

How is it with you? Does Christmas set you apart from, or make you a part of, a fellowship of all faiths? Does Christmas make the Christ more exclusive or inclusive in its appeal to spiritual understanding?

3.

Miracle

MEMORY, MEANING and MIRACLE. Without the wonder of the supernatural, the Advent season would lose its most persuasive charm. Miracles bear witness to God no less than to the power of the human mind to receive them.

MIRACLE is merely a religious term for what to God must be "a natural." All life is a miracle, for there *are* secrets hidden from us that continue to defy scientific *and* metaphysical explanation.

MEMORY and MEANING combine to assure us that the MIRACLE of Christmas is more than belief in a Virgin Birth, a Guiding Star, and an Angels' Song. All of these with their varied connotations in the far-flung field of Christian expression are still only part of the "divine imperative."

Now, if we could but demonstrate PEACE — the most needed miracle in our modern time, the yet unrealized MIRACLE which was so vividly prophesied by Isaiah when he described the coming Christ as the Prince of Peace.

We harp on this each Christmas, but never more urgently than now. We have our sporadic waves of hope and faith and watch them wash away. But at this Christmas, in these incredible years targeted on Century 21, many of us are persuaded that we might — by sheer necessity or grace of God, by serendipity or the fact that there is no longer an alternative — take an inter-global chance on the life and teachings of the Man called Jesus.

I often wonder, has Christianity itself made Isaiah's Prince of Peace too exclusively Christian? Too institutionalized, too subordinate to life beyond life, instead of life here and now, too much a PRINCE OF PEACE in man's image rather than in the image and likeness of God?

Well, as we said earlier, "Christmas is a great idea, but it takes time." When you think how difficult it is to settle even a family quarrel and how sometimes even *Christians* can't settle domestic differences, we should, perhaps be more patient with quarrels among religions and international ideological conflicts in the world.

It shouldn't have taken 2,000 years, however, to persuade us to think seriously in global terms of the "miracle of a peace," but it has. It should have come quicker, but it didn't. It should have been obvious, but it wasn't. There is still time, though Christmas comes but once a year. And, oh, how stealthily!

Like many another, I have come into this consciousness about peace in our time all too slowly. In my growing-up years when my particular evangelical denomination was dedicated to the aims and goals of "the church militant," I was drafted into its ranks. I remember the fervor with which we used to sing, "Onward Christian soldiers, marching as to war, with the cross of Jesus going on before!"

More shocking, now that I think of it, was the hymn, "The Son of God goes forth to war, his kingly crown to gain; His blood-red banner streams afar! Who follows in his train?"

Wanting toy soldiers or a BB gun for Christmas was bad enough, but to put the Prince of Peace at the head of an army "marching as to war" was, as I think of it now, devastating.

Whether or not we believe in miracles or hope for proof of the miraculous, at Christmas give me, *Hark! the Herald Angels Sing* or *Oh, Come All Ye Faithful.* Or, for the sake of a good old touch of American sentimentality, as forward-looking and traditional as the honor accorded the Statue of Liberty and closely related to its spirit, give a thought to Longfellow's,

"I heard the bells on Christmas Day
Their old familiar carols play,
And wild and sweet the words repeat,
Of peace on earth, good will to men!

"But in despair I bowed my head,
There is no peace on earth, I said,
For hate is strong and mocks the song
Of peace on earth, good will to men.

"Then pealed the bells more loud and deep,
God is not dead, nor doth He sleep!
The wrong shall fail, the right prevail,
With peace on earth, good will to men!

"Then, ringing, singing on its way,
The world revolved from night to day,
A voice, a chime, a chant sublime,
Of peace on earth, good will to men!"

Christmas is a time to build a consciousness of peace, to work toward peace, to affirm peace, to demonstrate it in personal relationships, and to believe in its MIRACLE.

There have been many examples of the use of the tools of peace by which settlement of serious differences were negotiated without the conflict of arms. From a William Penn to a Gandhi to a Martin Luther King, there are evidences that widespread armed conflicts can be resolved by other means than terrorism and bloodshed. The power of love and reason inherent in the philosophy of the Prince of Peace has always succeeded where it has truly been tried.

High on the picturesque mountainous border between Chile and Argentina stands a colossus, made of melted cannon. With right hand upraised in a sign of peace and blessing and left hand bearing an uplifted cross, the 26-foot figure commemorates the 1903 settlement of a bitter boundary dispute between the two South American nations.

The plaque reads, "Sooner shall these mountains crumble into dust, than the people of Argentina and Chile break the peace they have sworn to maintain at the feet of Christ the Redeemer." A railway tunnel beneath the statue connects the two countries, and each Christmas particular reference, homage, and remembrance are paid to the miracle-working power of *El Cristo de Los Andes*.

By way of MEMORY, MEANING and MIRACLE, the Christ in whatever language challenges the world that His message of PEACE ON ÉARTH, GOOD WILL TO MEN become part of humanity's life and thought as we contemplate the memory of the CHRISTMAS CHILD, the meaning of MESSIANIC HOPE, and the miracle of the PRINCE OF PEACE.

Sometime during the Advent season, preferably many times, find a quiet place, and in the spirit of meditation listen to what MEMORY has to tell you about past Christmases and your spiritual growth.

Sometime during the Yuletide period set aside some moments when, without disturbance, you discover what conclusions you have reached about the MEANING of

Christmas, and ask yourself what you are doing with the MEANING.

Sometime during the Christmastide and in your periods of meditation in the coming year, review where you stand in regard to the workability of the MIRACLE — the message of the Prince of Peace — and ask yourself where and how you can possibly help hasten the actualization of the yet unrealized dream.

Chapter Three

Monsieur Minuit

MONSIEUR MINUIT

A Vignette

    Having often advocated that the most selfless way of giving is to give anonymously, I have frequently put the preachment into practice. Then I discovered that my greatest reward was in thinking back on an anonymous gift and wanting to talk about it! While this may rob it of its virtue, there is one such occasion that may be shared simply because of Christmas.

It happened once upon a time in *gai Paree* when I gave away a poodle, a French poodle, obviously, and about the cutest *chien* I had ever seen. Black as a lump of coal, with a pompon tail, it sported a cute white collar set with rainbow colored gems. His name was *Minuit* (Midnight), and he was not quite six months old. A Parisian friend, who had tipped me off on this opportunity for my good deed, delivered the puppy to its new mistress, Jacqueline. This young lady was nine, and for the past four years had not been able to walk because of polio. I had never seen this *jeune fille*, and outside of the fact that she lived on the Boulevard St. Germain where her widowed mother rented rooms to students and worked as a seamstress, I had no more information. I only knew that Jacqueline wanted nothing more in all the world than a poodle, a *caniche*. Evidently her reception of the gift surpassed any joy she had experienced in a long time. A mental picture of her in her chair, her face registering a gasp of wonder as she clasped *Minuit* in her arms, put an instant picture into my heart as well, and I was ready to evangelize once more on the merit of anonymous deeds.

The day after the presentation of the gift, when I left the Rue de la Fontaine where I was staying, Paris never looked more wonderful. The Eiffel Tower was more impressive, the Arc de Triomphe more *triomphant*, the lovers in the Jardin des Tuileries and along the Seine more amorous. I drove to Fontainebleau that day and never had the forest been so enchanting or the hundreds of bicyclists less annoying. I attributed these good feelings and good fortune to *Monsieur Minuit*.

On the following morning, however, I was roused at an early hour by the jangle of the telephone beside my bed. It was a call from the friend, who had arranged *l'affaire anonyme*, informing me excitedly that it had turned into an *affaire tragique*. *Monsieur Minuit* was gone. Apparently he had gotten out of Jacqueline's apartment and, heeding the call of the out-of-doors, had gone adventuring. Jacqueline, too stunned to cry, had insisted on being taken outside in her wheel chair where she searched the *quartier* with hands clasped as if praying, which she undoubtedly was. The police had been notified.

"Why," I asked myself, "do these things happen?" A person can rationalize himself out of almost any situation, and I have a predilection for doing just that, usually coming up on the Lord's side by saying, "There must be a deeper meaning somewhere in all this," but just now I certainly could not see one. All I could think was that the poodle was wandering in the Paris traffic of which there is none worse in the world, with the possible exceptions of Tokyo or Rome or Los Angeles or New York. Any city street could mean sudden and certain death for a *caniche*, pompon tail or no pompon tail.

I tried my hand and heart at affirming positive divine protection of *Minuit*. Having advocated this to other people who were in difficult straits, I realized again how easy it is to emphasize it until one is called upon to bring it to bear personally. "Think positive thoughts about Midnight," I told myself, but asked, "do you have the will to believe them in the light of realistic reasoning?" At any rate, I compelled myself to paraphrase one of my favorite affirmations:

> The light of God surrounds you, *M'sieur Minuit,*
> The love of God enfolds you,
> The power of God protects you,
> The presence of God watches over you;
> Wherever you are, *M'sieur Minuit,* God is!

Then came a pleading call from my friend. Wouldn't I drop around and talk to Jacqueline? She was determined to meet the donor of the dog, and wouldn't it be wonderful if I went over and we commiserated together, perhaps even arranging for a replacement of Midnight?

Still wondering about the deeper meaning of all this and asking myself why a girl's joy should be turned into grief, and whether my anonymous act was a wise one in the first place, I went to Jacqueline's home. Never had the traffic been more annoying or the lovers along the Seine more inane.

Only dog lovers know what it is like to lose a dog, and only those who believe in affirmations will appreciate how I felt when I neared the Boulevard St. Germain. My eyes searched out every wheel-free spot of road and every visible bit of grass and curbing to see whether there might be a bundle of black moving about or lying silently alone, unmoving.

Reaching the house, I ruefully asked the concierge how to reach Jacqueline's room. As he gave me directions, he shook his head sorrowfully and interspersed, "Terrible about the *chien* — he was such a lovely one — but his blackness made him impossible to see — now take a white poodle or even a pink one — ."

Sadly I walked up the three flights to the accompaniment of radios blaring in several rooms. Jacqueline's mother met me at the door, excitedly and in tears, taking me immediately into the room where Jacqueline was crying as I had never seen a girl cry before, tears of laughter, tears of joy, while snuggled in her arms was *Monsieur Minuit*.

He had just been found, whimpering in a hallway closet where he had evidently strolled the previous night, before the door blew shut or somehow closed on him mysteriously.

"Didn't he bark immediately or during the night?" I asked.

"He did not make one sound," Jacqueline boasted. "He is such a brave one! Or do you think he cried *un peu?* "

"I should think he cried a little," I chimed in. "He must have done some deep thinking in that closet, don't you suppose, thinking about the way things happen in this world of ours!"

"I knew he would come back!" Jacqueline assured me through her ecstatic tears, "I knew he would. Do you not have such feelings, monsieur, when you just *know?* "

Midnight stuck out his bobbing red tongue. I stroked his curly black head.

"Sometimes I do have such feelings, Jacqueline," I confessed. "Sometimes I do."

Because of Christmas, I let it stand at that.

Chapter Four

Nostalgia

NOSTALGIA

1.

"*Nostalgia*: A wistful longing for something long ago and far away that is actually nearer than we think. Example: Christmas." So says my private, unexpurgated dictionary!

At no time more than during the Advent season are we persuaded to look back into the past and forward into the future while often overlooking our present blessings. Nostalgia, thy name is Janus. Janus, the mythological two-faced guardian of the portals of the beginning and the end of things, seemed quite unconscious of the wonder of what was happening in between.

But, at that, the two-way view can be of help. Rightly interpreted, nostalgia can put our world into a clearer perspective and alert us to the fact that remembered joys are never past, though some joys seem too good to last. The nostalgia often felt so keenly during the Advent period can help us space things out so that we recognize what we have to be thankful for. And that's where Christmas plays its role.

The Yuletide season, which means the winter solstice, used to plunge me into deep feelings of loneliness and a kind of homesickness — nostalgia. It bothered me, this secret sense of yearning, until I realized it wasn't a secret at all. It was, in fact, quite universal. Almost everyone seemed to have had it during the Christmastide, just like he or she had had the common cold or whatever else was going around.

Even the ancient Greeks and Romans had it — nostalgia — and that is why they staged their winter solstice festivals as a therapy for their needs, all of which was long before Christmas ever appeared on the scene.

I could identify with these early animistic worshipers. The very fact that the days were getting shorter, as if the sun was tired, often got through to me. "There goes another year," I mused nostalgically. And it didn't help matters when the merchandisers and the religionists started an Advent clamor that everybody should be Christmas happy even though Planet Earth *was* getting drab.

Deeper went the moodiness of us who suffered the malaise called nostalgia, and psychiatrists warned it could go into nostomania. There was no drug on the market for what ailed us (thank heaven), and the pharmaceutical cartels had no way of dealing with the cause and cure of this phenomenon (twice thanks to heaven). Thrown upon our own resources we had to figure out a treatment for ourselves. Suddenly to some, and gradually to others, a revelation and a cure crept into our consciousness: an awareness typical of the American Way and the style in which we do things, not always fully understood by the world at large, not always clear, but comparable to the dramatization and honor paid to Lady Liberty in her centennial year. We celebrated as if we had suddenly discovered her greatness, her meaning, and her mission. She had been there all along, torch in hand, but never quite honored so unanimously and in depth. Just so, through twenty centuries, the Christmas spirit relights a star, reunites a Christian world, and celebrates its miracle of faith.

At last we had our nostalgia diagnosed. When we asked ourselves at Christmas time, "What are we nostalgic *for?* What is this longing for some long ago something all *about?*" the answer was clear: *We felt in our heart of hearts that Christmas was becoming more and more a realizable dream of what we and the world could be like if the transitory spirit of Christmas could be perpetualized.*

We were once more being tantalized by the utopian vision of a Christmas all year long! We had, of course, gone through this before in endless years gone by, 2,000 years, in fact, and our Janus-faced mythological seer was telling us that we had better get it done before Star Wars and Armageddon put us all out of business. He was again seeing only the beginning and the end.

Nostalgia, now that it was understood as both cause and cure, took on a new perspective. The greatest thing about Christmas, we realized, was that, since it *did* come once a year, it persuaded the sun to once more rise and shine, and then passed on. The newest thing about Christmas is that because it was simply an annual affair, it had never grown

45

old. Its most challenging feature was that, individually and collectively, it once more challenged us, did not impose itself upon us overly-long, and kept just the proper psychological distance between us and its omnipotence, so that we both felt comfortable.

Its goals, in terms of peace, mother and child, joy, freedom, immortal love and global good will, were definitely *eternal verities*. The hope of Christmas, ages old, became more contemporary with each passing year. Forever young, forever enchanting, could we really stand it, would we truly appreciate it if it became a *daily* routine affair of the heart? A year-round Christmas? We couldn't take it.

I had to conclude: It is nostalgia itself that makes each Christmas sacred and singing! It is nostalgia that keeps the Star alive and shining in the Yuletide sky.

2.

Of Christmas Cards and Greetings

Especially fascinating during the Advent season is the endless variety of cards and round-robin family letters. It is wonderful what the people on our ever-growing, ever-changing Christmas lists come up with in the way of holiday greetings. Reverence and humor, sentiment and satire, art and artifice, you name it, we get it, and so do you. More than that, each message tells us something about the lifestyle of the senders, and even more about ourselves in our reactions to this inundating flow of the surging Christmas*tide*. At this particular point, nostalgia becomes a therapy, and the exchange of greetings is unquestionably good for the soul.

This annual outpouring assures us that no matter where fortune has taken us and our far-flung Christmas friends during the rapidly closing year and, out of touch though we may have been, time is a river and we are now back together, all in the same boat on another Christmas cruise. This is why cards and letters should be as upbeat and hope-inspired as possible, the better for all of us to enjoy and survive another Advent trip.

Since both the cause and the cure for nostalgia are involved in the exchange of greetings, a light and lively philosophical touch is recommended. Joy, as the saying has it, is not true joy until it is shared, and sorrow is not true sorrow unless it is borne alone. Like all axioms, this saying is open to debate, but it may help direct us in the phrasing and direction of our "Merry Christmasing."

Our particular practice has been to personalize our greetings by way of Lorena's photocraft. For more than twenty years her darkroom has been the source for processing new light on Christmas as we see it.

Greeting card companies have never objected to people doing their own thing with their own original ideas. Why should they? Latest count on the number of commercial Christmas cards annually sold and mailed in the U.S.A. and Great Britain put the figure at more than one billion. 1,000,000,000! That's a lot of mailbags! More than enough to test the faith and strength of those "whom neither snow, nor rain, nor heat, nor gloom of night can stay from the swift completion of their appointed rounds."

The Christmas card idea goes back to 1845. It was then

that Queen Victoria's favorite painter, W. C. Dobsen, came up with the first Yuletide card, said by some to have been simply a candle and a wreath. (*This was the year following the first telegraphic message sent by inventor Morse from Washington to Baltimore saying, "What hath God wrought!"*) The Dobson card was lithographed, and copies were sent to friends of both the artist and the Queen. Why? Because of a nostalgia for sharing at this holy time of year and, no doubt, to show off the artist's art.

As might have been expected, in the following year, 1846, the recipients of the Dobson card reciprocated in kind. They, too, had artist friends and poets whose talents *they* wished to share. (*This was the year prior to 1847, the year the first stick-on stamp was invented in the U.S.A. Benjamin Franklin's imprint cost a nickel, George Washington's a dime.*)

So grew the idea of keeping in touch, because of Christmas. Wars, famines, earthquakes, and warnings of Armageddon couldn't dislodge the growing custom of sending cards during Advent and buying adhesive stamps to get the greetings into the mail. Today Christmas would hardly be Christmas without the flood of special cards and special Christmas stamps. The custom has become so much a part of our culture, our consciousness, our sentimentality and our merchandising, that even Scrooge-oriented corporations and agnostic consortiums salute their friends and clientele with, "God rest you merry, gentlepersons, Let nothing you dismay!"

Dismay most often occurs
    when someone on the list is missed.
This causes stress
    until a new card is addressed.
But now with computers and the laser ray
    high tech gadgets save the day!

The point is that *the cause and the cure of nostalgia are alternative modes in our state of mind.*

Telephone and telex
    can carry your carols day or night
    — by satellite —
With love and blessings generously unfurled
    in a momentarily changed and friendly
    Christmas world.

3.

Out of the Darkroom — Into the Mails

First there was Bethlehem. Bethlehem is more than a town or city. It is a concept.

It may be the highest and deepest concept of man's dream of peace, born first within himself, projected into society, extended around the world.

Lorena's picture speaks for itself. It tells its own story. Despite the wars that have swept the Middle East, the religions that have stood divided over the meaning of Him who came into being here, and the days and nights when guns have sounded, there is a time when one instinctively wants to say, "Oh little town of Bethlehem, how still we see thee lie. Above thy deep and dreamless sleep, the silent stars go by." To wise men and shepherds alike, this ancient village of Judea with its now 30,000 residents is still "the House of Bread", symbolic of spiritual sustenance and the fellowship of faith.

Rest easy, Bethlehem, and don't give up the dream!

4.

Christmas is joy, fun, and the remembrance of our kinship with all life. In our home at Christmas time, nostalgia calls for a creche with the traditional cast of characters — the Holy Family, wise men, shepherds, camels, sheep, manger cattle.

Close at hand in our home, as perhaps in yours, there is a pet or two, and one Christmas, long ago, our wire-haired terrier asked to be stuffed into a stocking and hung on the tree, but only for a moment.

Strange and wonderful, how innocent little things, especially animals who are "born free," trigger moments of deepening thought. We humans seem to be desperately dependent on the news media to keep us informed, on medicine to keep us well, and on legal counsel to keep us straight. Yet here, while spending Christmas week in our British Columbia cabin, we found a fawn prepared to make its way in the world without any of our sophisticated assists. It merited a Christmas recognition and a prayer:

Dear Father, hear and bless,
Thy beasts and singing birds;
And guard with special tenderness,
Small things that have no words.

5.

By virtue of our work, we tried our best to spend Christmas in so-called "foreign countries" only to find that the word "foreign" is no longer a tenable word and should be scrapped. Planet earth is, in actuality, a rather "small, small world."

At this very moment, somewhere on an ancient road people are walking, traveling, working. It may not be a Christian Christmas time for non-Christian people, but the spirit of the period, the cosmological, seasonal, spiritual awareness is there just the same.

Yuletide is a universal recognition of the nature of birth and rebirth. The ancient road is every road, and, remembering this, we can better feel ourselves a part of God's world, walking our own path of faith more understandingly.

Lorena caught scenes that told the story graphically. It is only separation from others that makes the road seem lonely. Participation and sharing, even if only in mind, brings all life into clearer focus.

Walk with people in thought and you walk more thoughtfully with Self.

> Wherever you are, people of the world,
> Wherever you walk, people of God,
> Wherever you travel, children of men,
> Merry Christmas!

6.

There is something in the heart of us that wants a shrine, a focal point for the spirit. It may be someone to love and admire or it may be nothing more than a memory to which we return nostalgically for reassurance. You may not even wish to call the precious still-point in your life a "shrine," but every secret longing has its homing place.

At Christmas, shrines need no apology or explanation. It may be Bethlehem or a Christmas tree or a lighted candle in a darksome room. Churches, chapels, cathedrals, wayfare stations, rescue shelters, all are crowded at Christmas time, and all are "Shrines."

This one stood alone and told its own silent story. It represented something deep and personal within oneself, as if it were a picture of the "Saint" in us playing a game with God.

This last picture, incidentally, took infinite patience. Try it sometime and see how difficult it is to train the wildlings to be in their right places at the right time — and smile!

An English parody suggests that there may be a greater affinity between us and our feathered friends than we care to admit:

"The Christmas muse, her annual theme rehearses,
To tell us birds are singing in the sky.
But if the shoppers slam their doors with curses,
You can bet the little sparrows wonder why!

"But if you are calm and keep the Christmas time in stride,
And let your heart be somewhat light and free,
Then even birds will flutter at your side,
And light in pairs — or sometimes even three."

7.

Here was a Christmas gift, beautifully cast in bronze, a jug-girl who during the photographing was upstaged by a squirrel getting a headstart on winter. It was all too good not to share with friends who know the fun and joy and blessing of the Christmastide.

8.

Then there was the year (1968) marked by the miracle of the Apollo flight, an event that momentarily thrilled and unified the world, making us more at home in the universe-at-large.

Lorena maneuvered us snuggly into our Christmas tree space capsule, succeeding in capturing the grand idea through the camera lens. Added inspiration was supplied when Elizabeth Landeweer gave us permission to use her remarkable poem, *Christmas Ball*, for our Christmas card greeting:

"Viewed from some point high over all,
Our earth looks like a Christmas ball,
A brilliant bauble of the air;
One handles Christmas balls with care,
For they are fragile and may break;
But we have learned our earth can take
The lightning and the thunderbolts
And all of time's successive jolts
And still remain serene in place.
"Not every child when he is small
Is given his own Christmas ball
Of burnished gold and green and blue;
And, Father, we are children, too;
We sometimes stumble in our play,
And though the earth is ours today,
I think of dawns like rosy glass,
And frail white blossoms in the grass,
And I go down upon my knees,
And whisper, 'Handle gently, please.' "

"Let's read it again before we get back to work," Lorena suggests, and I am more than game, especially when she adds with sly flattery, "You memorized it, way back when."

It is all the urging I need to blend nostalgia with the miracle of Christmas and the marvel of a lunar conquest.

We stay for a moment in thought. Life does have its miracles in the fields of both science and religion, and a growing agreement suggests that the two have more in common than in conflict. "Miracles" in either area are but the discovery of the working of immutable laws. Every breakthrough, whether on the lunar surface or in the inner mind, brings us nearer to this truth.

Of Time and Tide

Our moments with the Christmas album might have then ended but for my random turning of the pages. My eyes fell on the earliest "family portrait" of Lorena and me which we used shortly after we had started our "made in the darkroom" annual greetings. The year was 1959, and the picture was built around the homespun couplet:

"**Christmas cards bring Yuletide cheer,
Enough to last throughout the year!**"

It was also a show-off of cards we had received the previous year, and an attempt to use the magic of the delayed shutter release to determine whether Lorena could get into the picture in time without looking uncomfortably hurried.

Years later (1973) we created a summer scene that won
an award as a symbol of "What's Right with the World":

> The out-of-doors,
> The open sky;
>   An unspoiled lake,
>   A love of life,
>   Remembering friends
>   At Christmas time.

9.

The years go by. Nostalgia deepens as one looks back. Christmas greetings, whether sent or received, constitute a diary of time and tide. Successes, sorrows, highs and lows, acclaims and disclaimers, great expectations and mystifications, things revealed and things concealed, smooth sailing and stormy weather, pets to have and hold, and pets now gone, but remembered — life is a delayed shutter on an infallible camera....

I turn the album pages, and it is 1981. In that year, despite a hunch that our Christmas list family might have had enough of "family portraits", we couldn't resist opening the doors on my finally realized dream of a beautifully constructed workshop two floors up and as private as a penthouse. Christmas was the time for its christening. I thought of calling it my TREE HOUSE or ALONE AT LAST or THE HEIGHT OF FOLLY or SALAD DAYS, after Shakespeare's phrase of the time of youth and inexperience. But being of a more intentioned turn of mind, we settled for THE UPPER ROOM.

10.

Decembers come and Decembers go, and last Christmas serendipity had us ticketed for another "Christmas at Home" photo finish. The house had been newly painted and the lawn was neatly trimmed, and we thought it would be fun to test our agility to get into the scene in keeping with the automatic shutter magic. We both tried it and were well rewarded.

But as I review the pictures in sequence and examine the "family shots" perceptively, I have to say, "That may be part of the nostalgia."

"What do you mean?" Lorena asks.

I point to the photos. I get a magnifying glass. I look at her. She looks at me. We look at the pictures together.

"Well, now, wait a minute," she says when I call attention to the corroding effect of time. "I don't think we have changed *that* much!" She snaps the album pages back to 1973 when she had me up a tree, and says, "I'll bet you could still climb up there as easily today and trigger the shutter release as cleverly as you did then!"

Nostalgia. Because of Christmas we find a special closeness to loved ones and friends and remembrances played back for us on the reel of mind. We tell ourselves that if time corrodes, it also caresses. We get philosophical. "You're not growing old, you're just not as *young* as you used to be....those aren't wrinkles, they're character lines....you haven't changed a bit unless you *think* you have....don't you really feel younger *at heart?*"

"Nostalgia: A longing for something long ago and far away that is actually nearer than we think. Example: Christmas!"

Chapter Five

Creativity

CREATIVITY

1.

Of Love and Christmas

Next to "I LOVE YOU," few expressions of endearment are more meaningful than "MERRY CHRISTMAS!"

Yet, it is interesting to consider that "I LOVE YOU" is appropriate at any time of the year, but if you suddenly said, "MERRY CHRISTMAS!" in June or July, you might conceivably get some concerned reactions and be referred to an analyst.

The point is that though love and Christmas are among the best known concepts in the Christian faith and though both are virtue words of the highest order, Christmas is love enshrined around a specific time, place, and person. December 25 is the time. A manger is the place. The person is the Christ, or, if you prefer, the Child Jesus.

The paradox and wonder of all this is that when the Christmas spirit begins to overwhelm the world, as it does at the start of the Advent season, love and Christmas join ranks in a special way, non-Christian faiths feel the impact, and a surge of creativity reflects itself from cultural arts to commercial marketplace. There is always something new at Christmas, and be it a toy or treasure, it is greeted with a touch of love.

Because of Christmas, the phenomenon outreaches time and place. There is a rush of time, but also a sense of timelessness, a hint that the manger is everywhere, in every place, and that the "person" is enshrined in each of us in a very special way.

This awareness inspires a sudden sense of originality. From children to nonagenarians, the Christmas artist appears, even if only in the matter of wrapping gifts or decorating the tree or frosting the cake. Christmas, especially through the eyes of art and artists, stirs up whatever hidden genius or unrealized potential may be our own.

Externalizing the Christmas Story

When it comes to an understanding of the spirit of Christmas, we owe fully as much to art and artists as we do to churches and theologians.

Theologians perpetuated the reality of Christmas, musical composers immortalized its spirit, artists eternalized the dream. Religionists formulated the beliefs and rituals, the secular world enshrined creeds and cathedrals to match imagined cities of God.

No one today knows exactly when Jesus was born, and there has always been a question as to where His birth took place.

As to dogmatic details of the miraculous story, theologians debated long and hard about the obvious differences in Biblical accounts and scanty on-the-scene observances.

The Holy Family — Rembrandt

Religions have been split, denominations have remained stubbornly divided as to their respective interpretations. Dialectic battles have been waged about the Virgin Birth, the paternity of Jesus, the nature of the Star, the coming of the Wise Men, the shepherds, the manger, the Heavenly Hosts.

No matter. Creative artists, as if knowing that life, love and Christmas are beyond words or argumentation or dogmatic finding out, reached into the heart of "the greatest story ever told" and transmuted the seemingly unknown into a living part of humankind's esthetic relationship to God.

They, too, idealized the real so that we might realize the ideal. They brought the players in the divine drama to life, identified their roles, portrayed them with qualities and passions found within ourselves.

They enshrined them in ethereal beauty, and we came to know them, not necessarily as they really were, but as they are for *us*, for us who had the wish and the will to believe in the miracle of Christmas and a creative power within ourselves.

We owe these geniuses a debt for closing the gap between specula- tion and conviction. Did Mary truly look like this Madonna? Was the Infant Jesus really such a halo-vested child? Could Joseph have been a man so unas- suming and inno- cent of charm? Were there really cherubs winging, singing in the sky?

Nativity — David

So what! The artist with an inner vision portrayed the Miracle with a psychic touch. That which unfolded on the canvas was fashioned in the mind. The spiritual was meta- morphosed into the material without losing its state of grace. The fantasy became our fascination, filled our need, mirrored our imagination, persuaded us that this is how we might have sketched and painted *our* imagery had we but had the creative genius.

Their greatest contribution was to make us feel we had a part in creating these majestic masterworks. In a strange and wonderful way, we were there as the forms unfolded, as the figures grew, and as the mathematical magic of divine art came to life. *We were there.*

Adoration of the Magi — Quentin Massys

The Artist in You

How would the "artist in you" have portrayed the face and features of the Mother of Jesus? How would you have visualized her from what you had heard, read, and felt about her by way of love at "Christmas time"?

If you reviewed volumes of books and looked at the many celebrated paintings, which would you choose? I have just finished doing this very thing. Lorena, who photographed the paintings for this chapter, selected forty masterworks — paintings old and new, art works of the annunciation, the birth, the flight into Egypt — and spread them out so we could select the most compelling portrait of "The Virgin."

Madonna of the Rock — da Vinci

How difficult to choose or judge! How presumptuous to select one masterpiece from masterpieces! But eventually we settled for da Vinci's *Madonna of the Rock*. This print is but a detail of the oil on canvas painting featured in the Paris Louvre. In its entirety the scene presents Mary in a dazzling, yet shadowy cave with the Christ Child. Here, breathlessly inspiring, serene, and powerful, Virgin and Child are shown in a most profound and extraordinary setting. The pillars of rock, the lights and shadows, the mystery, all draw attention to the face and inner reflection of Mary as many Christians imagine her to be.

Adoration of the Shepherds — Catena

"Now when Jesus was born in Bethlehem of Judea in the days of Herod the king, behold, wise men from the East came to Jerusalem, saying, 'Where is he who has been born King of the Jews? For we have seen his star in the East, and have come to worship him.'

"When they saw the star, they rejoiced exceedingly with great joy, and going into the house, they saw the child with Mary his mother, and they fell down and worshiped him. Then, opening their treasures, they offered him gifts, gold and frankincense and myrrh." (Matthew 2:1-2; 10-11)

73

Madonna of the Book — **Botticelli**

Although we are devoting ourselves to the greatest classical works, let's recognize that every artist who was inspired by the Christmas message, from the most classical to those whose works are almost impossible to classify, has put something of his or her own culture, conditioning, and reach of heart and mind into the faces and figures of the Christmas cast of characters.

Madonna and Child — **Fra Felippo Lippi**

The most popular subject was "Madonna and Child." Even though not reproduced here in color, they challenge the imagination and cause us to experience once more the phenomenon of synchronicity, a feeling of oneness with the art and artistry that lies at the source of Christmas love and creativity.

And that is also why there is less argument, dissension, and debate about art presentations than there is about theological pronouncements. Works of Christmas art are mirrors reflecting our tastes, our wishes, and our needs. Classical Christmas art represents the consciousness of the good, the true, and the beautiful in us, born anew according to our knowing, our awareness, and our dreams.

Madonna of the Meadow — **Bellini**

A Learning Thought

There *is* an artist and an artistry in each of us, and Christmas is the inspiration we need to prove the truth of it.

Our art may not lie in painting masterworks or composing chorals or carols or carving a Madonna out of stone, but there are other tantalizing talents responsive to the Christmas time.

For example: the art of forgiveness or the art of forgetting a wrong and remembering a right..... the art of loving where love is needed..... doing the unexpected..... the art of appreciating art..... or blessing a friend or, better, an enemy..... or simply saying in a new and special way, "Thank you, Father, for Christmas."

True Art Is To Inspire Art

Among the famous immortals I hope to meet when, and if, I ever get to where the immortals are, is Michelangelo Buonarroti. Here was a genius who could endow a piece of marble with a touch of life, not unlike the touch of God when He "formed us out of dust."

That is why I went to Florence, or *Fierenze*, as the Italians call it, where Michelangelo was born on March 6, 1475. Here, because of his mother's illness, the child was put to nurse with a marble-worker's wife. "I sucked in the passion of my art," Michelangelo used to say, "along with my foster mother's milk."

It was snowing when I drove into the city on a February

77

night, and Florence looked like a story book town on Christmas Eve. The flakes were large and soft in falling, as if bending an ear to the weather report that predicted snow would all be gone by morning. But now, in mid-evening, it was blessing Florence with the first real snowfall in twenty years.

I wound my way through the narrow streets to the Plaza Lucchesi hotel on the banks of the Arno. People everywhere were in a holiday mood. True, the weather had been cold and the winter overly severe, but the snow was festive. The man who helped me with my luggage called it a "warm snow," saying that scores of people had gathered on the bridges that afternoon to photograph the white swans as they floated in the Arno amid the snow.

From my room I could see the darkly shimmering river wending its way on the other side of the stately parapet. Beyond, on the distant hills, rows of city lights twinkled as if to indicate a kind of victory over the gentle storm. But what was most intriguing was a group of youngsters — *ragazzi* — just below my window, gaily rolling the snow into huge balls and lugging them to the parapet where they proceeded to create their snow-sculptured figures. With expert skill one of the trio outdid the others, both by speed of his execution and by his artistry. Perched on the parapet, this *ragazzo*, wearing a feather in his close-fitting cap, fashioned a Madonna while his young assistant tossed lumps of snow up to him. Quickly the Madonna took shape and, in the light of the street lamps, the figure looked for all the world like something hewn out of marble.

Passersby, fascinated by the young *artista*, stopped to watch. Soon they began praising him with shouts of *"Bravo! Va benissimo! Stupendo!"* To which he laughingly replied, *"Grazie! Queste sono cose facili!"* (Thank you! This is all very easy!)

Umbrellas were quietly folded by the pedestrians, not only because the snow was letting up, but almost as if in respect for this youthful modern Michelangelo. Two snow-men, a snow dog, and a snow missile poised for launching competed for acclaim from the spectators, but the boy with the feather in his cap outdid them all with his Madonna to which he now added a child clasped in the semblance of motherly arms.

Surely the spirit of Michelangelo was on the street that night awakening within the viewers' hearts the hidden talent within themselves. Surely he was there, reliving again the details of his early life, his poverty, his struggle with himself, his faith in his destiny, his mastery as artist of the Medicis, his loneliness, his stubborn temper, and his will. I felt I saw him from my window, but when morning came there was nothing to be seen but shapeless mounds of melting snow on the parapet and water running in the streets.

The impromptu exhibition of a night of sculpturing was like a fantasy, rather like the dream of all of us who, if only for a little while, have our moments of creative fulfillment, brief moments, yet long enough to let us know that they are there, were there, at least, as part of our innermost expression: a *Moses* or a *David* by a Michelangelo, a snowman, or a snow Madonna by an unknown boy. What does it matter? Especially at Christmastime?

Chapter Six

Los Pastores

LOS PASTORES

Feliz Navidad

Age-old drama is relived each Christmas season among the adobe villages in the region of Santa Fe, New Mexico. Hispanics, Indians, and Anglo-Saxons gather in the plazas or out in the mountains to enjoy the reenactment of primitive plays, plays brought from Spain during the sixteenth century by the Conquistadores . . . who also brought a lust for conquest . . . and the long reach for power and gold. But, because of Christmas, the plays survive.

One of the oldest survivals is *Los Pastores* (*The Shepherds*), performed annually throughout the Southwest at periods ranging from the fiesta of Our Lady of Guadalupe, December 12, through to Twelfth Night, January 6.

Los Pastores is the story of the Judean shepherds, Spanish-style, who watching their flocks, hear the angel's song and decide to go to Bethlehem. This would be familiar treatment were it not for the inclusion of the Devil in the play and the personal appearance of Michael, the Archangel. Because of these additions to the character plot and certain other surprise elements, the play surpasses the general run of Christmas dramatizations.

It is the night before Christmas, and we are in the Sandia Mountains among a group of some fifty sightseers and an equal number of "natives." We have found places in the moonlit clearing where crude benches have been set facing the mountain slope. Several Indians, almost totally concealed in their *chimayos*, and a number of Mexican women, securely wrapped in *rebozos*, stand nearby. It is a silent night. The air is cool and enchanting. The "mountain-slope-stage" is in darkness. Occasionally a car is heard burrowing through a mountain pass.

Suddenly, without announcement, a far-distant song is sung in Spanish by men's voices. Quietly at first, as though coming out of the *arroyo*, the voices, untrained, echo through the hills.

In Bethlehem's holy manger
    There shines a wondrous light;
To save our souls from danger,
    The Saviour's born tonight.

March on together joyfully,
    While angels sing;
For our Lord's Nativity
    We tamales bring.

The song continues. We dimly perceive the group of shepherds. They carry staffs as an indication of their station. In attire they are like the Mexicans one sees every day throughout New Mexico. Two torches carried by shepherd lads light the scene.

The song evokes a strange spirit from a rock nearby. A spotlight, buried in the slope of the mountain and serving as a footlight, instantly reveals him. It is Lucifer, not easily mistaken with his serpentine tail, horns, satanic mask, and trident gripped fiercely in hand. While the song serves as a background and the shepherds pause conveniently some distance away, the evil one identifies himself.

What are these songs that pierce my ears?
What means this sacred sphere? These chants
Of praise, these sounds of joy today
That fill me with despair?

Is it possible, he mutters, that a Saviour has been born? Might the King of Heaven actually reveal himself to lowly shepherds? Highly irked, Lucifer swishes his tail.

The shepherds approach. The devil "vanishes" behind his rock. The shepherds sing:

> Gifts and songs we carry,
>> Faithful hearts we bring,
> Never long we tarry
>> When we seek our King.

The song is concluded as they reach the main acting area. They pitch camp, have something to eat, get a little rest, and then proceed to find the Christ.

Two new characters are now introduced: Gila, the servant girl who is to do the cooking; and a Hermit, dressed in white, representing the pietistic individual who is intent on finding *Messias* everywhere but within himself. He begs hospitality from the shepherds and is made welcome.

Simply and beautifully now, the spotlight dims and a campfire is lighted. As Senor Parrado is elected to stand watch, Senor Tebano sits nearby vocalizing for the great solo he is to sing in church the next day. Gila is ordered off to find some edibles, the Hermit is occupied with his thoughts, the other shepherds are dozing when suddenly an apparition appears. Against the sky, an Angel stands with lifted wings. He says that *Messias* is indeed born, but warns Parrado that Lucifer, lurking nearby, will attempt to thwart their pilgrimage.

PARRADO: Tabano, yonder,
            Shining bright,
            What a wonder,
            See! A Light!

Tebano is only mildly interested. The Angel flaps his wings and is blacked-out. The other shepherds, Bato, Bartolo, Nabal, and Meliso, are wakened.

Lucifer now appears, disguised as a traveler. He does not deceive us. The moment we see him emerge from his hiding place and his oily voice pleads for food, we are on to him. But the shepherds are almost taken in until a chance reference to the *Messias* makes them suspicious. The Hermit accosts the devil and demands to know his name. Thoroughly harassed, Lucifer vows to torment them with all his wiles and threatens to chase their souls into hell. The shepherds, cowering and afraid, are saved in the nick of time by the reappearance of the Angel who drives Lucifer off into the night.

Gila returns with baskets of food. The shepherds compliment her and prepare to eat their supper. Lazy Bartolo sends a young shepherd boy, Cucharon, to see if the flocks are safe.

Cucharon, whistling, jogs along with his staff when the devil leaps into his path. The boy, evidently knowing little about underworld personnel and caring less, says, *"Buenas Noches!"* Lucifer assumes an affable pose and begins to inquire about *Messias*: where He is to be born, whether the shepherds are setting out in search of Him soon, and what people in general are saying about the so-called Son of God. Cucharon thinks the devil is inquiring, not about *Messias*, but about a long-sought Cucharonian cousin whose name happens to be *Matias*. He answers the devil's question in this double meaning:

LUCIFER: Say, then, hast heard the gossips tell
                Of the Messiah's birth, or that
                He soon shall come?

CUCHARON: Oh sir, kind sir,
                Matias is my cousin.
                Two years ago, by accident,
                He slew a man, was banished for it,
                But later on they pardoned him.

The devil boils. Sputtering his disgust, he warns the lad that he will consume him with flames. Cucharon sinks to his knees. Lucifer advances with this trident raised to strike, and Cucharon calls on God. "That Name no devil can endure!" screams Lucifer, as he drops his trident and vanishes. Forgetting all about the safety of Bartolo's flocks or his own fears, Cucharon rushes back to the shepherd group. Wide-eyed he tells how he has seen the evil one. "Friends, I have seen the devil!" But Nabal has greater wonders to tell. The whole angelic host has appeared. Listen! "There's that celestial music now!" And from above the Sandia Mountains the hymn of praise proclaims *Messias'* birth.

We move into the climax of the drama. Lucifer, driven by the music, comes into the camp undisguised and unafraid. Death to the shepherds now! "Hell waits your souls!" A dazzling light breaks over the scene. The Archangel Michael descends into the camp. In majestic, sweeping passages he and Lucifer take over the action. Antagonist and protagonist come to grips. They engage in actual physical combat. With his bare hands Michael subdues the lord of the underworld. The trident is broken, and the evil one lies quivering at the Angel's feet.

MICHAEL: Vanquished art thou!
                And shalt behold thyself
                For greater punishment, bound down
                Forever with this chain!

LUCIFER: (*bewailingly*) Oh me!
                Could pain be greater? Shame and
                   rage,
                Why burst ye not my heart?
                            Michael,
                My spirit yields; that name alone
                Can vanquish me!

Our audience, which has seen the play year after year, knows this is but subterfuge. Scarcely has Michael turned his back and consoled the shepherds than Lucifer is summoning the legions of hell for succor. Devils rush in from everywhere, but Michael bars their path, unvexed and unafraid. He addresses the Prince of Devils.

> MICHAEL: What, Lucifer, thou lingerest still?
> Begone! and let the shepherds haste
> To see the Word made human flesh.
> Arise, thou loathsome beast, plunge down
> The yawning chasm, where damning sin
> Will prove itself thy sharpest pain!

Against the heavens, the Christmas Star appears. Michael points it out to Parrado and to Nabal. The devils have departed, and the path is clear. "Go, all of you, to Bethlehem. Take your tamales to the Saviour King."

Where the star appeared, the details of the manger are now illuminated. The songs of the shepherds are timed so that there is no break in the action when they all gather at the stall. A glowing light assures us of the presence of the long-sought *Messias*.

The action which follows is so beautiful, so characteristic, so gentle, that it supplies a captivating "return" from the climactic point. As the members of the company, each in turn, approach the crib, they explain their motives for coming, and do some promoting for the salvation of their souls and their earthly well-being at the same time. Thus, the Hermit quickly takes credit for the entire pilgrimage. He sings a song, then kneels to pray the *adoracion* of the self-righteous.

HERMIT: All slept, none watched for Thy advent,
           But I alone! alert and glad,
           I urged them on, I brought them here,
           Vouchsafe us welcome, gracious Lord.
                                (he extends a gift)

           A silversmith of Mexico,
           Our glorious country! made me this,
           A reliquary richly wrought.
           Take it, dear Mother, for thy Son,
           Behold on it the holy cross.
           'Twill hush the Baby when He cries!

Bato presents the Christ Child with a toy game and, when he is quite sure that *Messias* understands, he gives up his place to Meliso.

MELISO: (*addressing Mary*) Good woman, how
           dost thou today?
           And how thy husband? Has he work
           In plenty? See, my milking pail
           Is broken; he shall mend it straight.
           Last eve, as my good woman milked,
           The black cow beat her vicious hoof
           Sharp on the pail, and crash it went!

Angry I cried, "Good mother, faith!
If thus thou carest for my goods,
I'm like to barter goods for care!"
I have a sister widowed late,
She begs to tend thy little one,
She'd feed Him well on dun cow's milk,
The same's made brother Gabe so
stout.

The quaint, kind humor of *Los Pastores* in this manger sequence is inspiring in its light and lively touch. It prompts the lad Cucharon to waltz over to Mary and Joseph, singing:

Dancing and singing,
Like birds on a tree,
Joyfully bringing,
Tamales to thee!

To many young *hermanitos*, no less than to us at the moment, God is as human as that.

Bartolo has fallen asleep, too exhausted and weary to go to the manger. The group prevails on him to get up. It is his golden opportunity, and *Messias* is waiting.

BARTOLO: (*yawning*) If thou'rt so anxious for me
             to see the child,
             Bring him here. I'm not a god-father.

He turns over, half asleep.

NABAL: O, come and see the kindly ox,
                Warming his guest and Infant Lord!

BARTOLO: Indeed not I; he might prove fierce
                And gore me sadly with his horns.

MELISO: Come, thou shalt see the friendly ass,
                Munching his hay beside the ox.

BARTOLO: Not I, I hate to watch a feast
                When I get neither bite nor soup!

Enter Lucifer. He grabs Bartolo by his feet to drag him off to hell. The shepherd, convinced at last that he has been under the devil's influence, frees himself, rushes to the manger, and lays a handful of tamales at the Infant's feet.

BARTOLO: Poor gifts! O would that wealth were
                mine!

He makes an added contribution by singing the Christ Child to sleep.

Cucharon now remembers that he never did find the sheep. In sudden alarm, they all realize that it is getting late and that by this time the sheep have surely fallen into the arroyo. So:

Because of Christmas

> Adios, Aunt Mary!
> Adios, Uncle Jo!

The Holy Mother extends her hands and blesses them, their church, their country, and the world. "Happy are they who receive that benediction!"

Joyfully *los pastores* turn toward their camp, singing as they wander far into the Sandia Mountains and the night.

Chapter Seven

Somewhere, Somehow, Sometime

SOMEWHERE, SOMEHOW, SOMETIME

Because of Christmas

1. *SOMEWHERE* in life every thinking person comes upon his or her Bethlehem, the place of spiritual awareness.

2. *SOMEHOW* in life every reasoning person finds a meaning and mission for his place in the scheme of things.

3. *SOMETIME* in life sincerely seeking individuals feel the presence of God's love and grace within themselves.

Let's look at these three motivations of Christmas in more detail:

1.

Somewhere

"And Joseph also went up from Galilee, from the city of Nazareth, to Judea, to the city of David, which is called Bethlehem, because he was of the house and lineage of David, to be enrolled with Mary, his betrothed, who was with child." (Luke 2:4-5)

Bethlehem is many things. It is a man going to the holy city, a woman giving birth to a child, shepherds hearing voices in the sky, wise men following a star. *It is every person somewhere in life finding a place of spiritual encounter.*

Scholars have speculated that it was not necessary that Mary should have gone to Bethlehem to be registered inasmuch as Joseph was authorized to register for his family. They suggest that Mary, being an adventurous and aggressive person, *insisted* on accompanying him. Joseph resisted, forbade her to go, but her determination dominated. When food was packed for the trip, Mary prepared double rations, loaded the donkey with essentials for the arduous 125-mile journey, and said to Joseph, "Come along!"

In our post-women's lib era of pop psychology, we can hear a rousing chorus of, "Good going, Mary! Bless you for being you!" But there was another factor involved: *Destiny.* History at any point persuades us that *individuals at all times have been directed by something higher and greater than themselves on their way to their Bethlehem confrontation.*

In one of my earliest books, *The Circle of Faith*, I trace the inevitable "somewhere" in the lives of people whom I met in my research and whose paths crossed the path of the Christ.

One was a German peasant girl, Therese Neumann, devoutly Catholic. The "somewhere" where she had her Bethlehem experience was a hospital bed. I went to Konnersreuth, Germany, to get her story.

When she was a young girl she had served as a link in the chain of volunteers who formed a bucket brigade when a neighborhood fire endangered her entire West German village. Therese stood on a chair, hoisting pails of water to a man on a ladder. The flaming heat, the frenzied shouting for ever greater speed, made her hysterical. She fell headlong to the ground.

Because of head injuries and complications, she was told there was no hope of her ever regaining total health. Her early wish to become a missionary seemed doomed, especially when she began losing her sight. It was then she dedicated herself to prayer, fasting, and rigorous discipline, affirming her *power to suffer vicariously, taking upon herself the aches, pains, and burdens of others!* She became a stigmatist, developing bleeding wounds (stigmata) resembling those on the crucified body of Christ, wounds which some people believe to be supernaturally impressed upon the bodies of certain persons, including St. Francis of Assisi.

Some called Therese a religious fanatic, a neurotic, an exhibitionist. Then people began claiming they *were* experiencing healing miracles by transferring their illnesses and diseases to Therese! Of the stigmata, Therese said, "It is the evidence of the Christ presence in His passion and of His place in my life."

Far-fetched as this may be to many, the point is that there are various places and circumstances in which individuals come upon their "Bethlehem miracle experience." In the case of Therese, as she dwelled upon the miraculous birth of the Christ Child and contemplated His ministry, her mission became clear. She determined to emulate Him by taking upon herself the sicknesses of the world as He had taken upon Himself the world's sins and shortcomings. She admitted that the Christ filled her with a sentiment and an emotion much as Mary must have experienced when she found herself "chosen of God" in the Bethlehem story.

Another person I included in my study and speculation of divine confrontations was a young musician, an Alsatian named Albert Schweitzer. His first confrontation occurred during early boyhood in a meadow on a Sabbath morning when he was out bird hunting and heard the angelus ring, summoning people to prayer in the Lutheran church at Gunsbach where his father was the pastor. Putting down his slingshot, he vowed he would never again knowingly seek to destroy any of God's creatures.

Long before I met Albert Schweitzer in Strasbourg, I knew he was a man with a greatness that touched people, no matter what their faiths might be. He had a commitment for spiritual service that could not be questioned, a philosophy that came to be known as "a reverence for life." It was, to hear him tell it, an encounter with the Christ awareness that persuaded him to leave the comfort of his Alsatian homeland and lose himself, the better to find himself, in a mission to help and heal the sick and needy at Lambarene in the African jungle.

Here was a genius in the field of music, perhaps the greatest interpreter of Johann Sebastian Bach, also one of the world's most respected authorities on the life and thought of the poet Goethe. Theologian, philosopher, humanistic scholar, Schweitzer became most renowned for his work as a physician and surgeon, emulating what he felt was his call in his response to the Bethlehem Child and his own personal quest for the "historical Jesus."

After I visited Dr. Schweitzer in Lambarene and caught more of his spirit, many things which seemed so devastatingly important in the realm of dogma, religious politicking, and division among sectarian groups lost their significance. I, too, asked myself about the somewhere in my Bethlehem confrontations. As Therese Neumann had made of Christ "a sentiment and an emotion" that caused her to find her mission, so Schweitzer had determined to make the historical Jesus *a way of life*.

Then there was Shoghi Effendi, a Middle Eastern scholar and student of world affairs. He found his "Bethlehem somewhere" when he was called upon to exercise responsibility and leadership in the Bahai faith.

There was the Italian, Eugenio Pacelli, a law student. His "somewhere" happened on the way to his classroom one day when he felt confronted by a vision of Christ in a remarkable *Quo Vadis* ("Where are you going?") experience. He became Pope Pius XII.

And there was American Helen Keller, blind almost from birth. Her "Bethlehem" involvement came at that moment when her soul's cry of "Light! Give me light!" was answered by the mystical illumination of an inner presence. Her influence in giving courage and inspiration to audiences, particularly college students, is one of religion's greatest and truest American legends.

Others in my *Circle of Faith* had *their* honest convictions about the Bethlehem encounter and its meaning. They contended that Christ should be recognized as Savior, Messiah, Wayshower, Master Teacher, Redeemer of the World, and Prince of Peace. The point of agreement is that He was born and that SOMEWHERE we too hear his "Follow me," and we recall that for two thousand years, well, at least since Bethlehem, men and women have heard these words in their hearts . . . . and followed Him.

Small wonder that these experiences prompted me to conclude that I, too, was on a pilgrimage through the Holy Land of my own life and what I saw and did in this experience was up to me. It was my challenge to affirm that the *spirit* behind the physical aspect of things never dies, that *faith* remains imperishable and that there is a temple of life which rebuilds itself by using both *nature* and *time* as friendly partners in the process.

Where was the SOMEWHERE where *you* came upon *your* Bethlehem, the counterpoint of spiritual awareness where your life was changed?

2.

Somehow

"And she gave birth to her firstborn son and wrapped him in swaddling clothes, and laid him in a manger, because there was no place for them in the inn." (Luke 2:7)

If there is a SOMETIME, there is also a *SOMEHOW* in life by which each thinking person finds the meaning and mission for a personal commitment in the scheme of things. The Christmas narrative reminds us that a woman may find it in the birth of a child, a man in the recognition of an overpowering mission, a young person in the awareness of an innate talent, a seeker in a moment of self-discovery, a wanderer in a time of sudden, star-guided illumination.

For every person there is the search and for every thinking person the discovery. *Somewhere, somehow, it is part of life's adventure.* The commitment carries the mandate: At that point where your talent meets the needs of the world — that is where God wants you to be.

If you ever get discouraged and conditions tend to get you down, remember the SOMEHOW of Christmas and consider the Bethlehem story:

The inn was overcrowded, and narrators tell us that Joseph sought lodging with distant relatives, but every room in Bethlehem was filled to overflowing. On returning to the courtyard of the inn he was informed that the caravan stables, situated just below the inn, had been cleared of animals and cleaned up for the accommodation of lodgers. *Somehow,* some good guidance was at work!

Because of Christmas

Leaving the donkey in the courtyard, Joseph and Mary shouldered the bags of clothing and provisions and descended the stone steps to their lodgings below. They found themselves located in what had been a grain storage room. In front of the stalls and mangers, tent curtains had been hung, affording at least a semblance of privacy.

Before break of day, pangs of childbirth were in evidence and, with the help and ministrations of women travelers, Mary was delivered of a male child. Jesus of Nazareth was born into the world, was wrapped in swaddling clothes, and laid in a nearby manger. *Somehow*, by the doing of this, prophecy was fulfilled.

Pin down the mission and meaning of your life by establishing a sense of values. Establish these values by thinking in terms of SOMEHOW. *Somehow* God *is* good, and God's good is for you and for the world at large.

Visual imagery, or picturization, as it is often called, imprints upon the mind a high and serviceable calling, leads to inner self discovery and, somehow, serves as a guide to your eventual place in life.

Mary had "dreamed a dream." Like her, *when we idealize the real, it is more possible to realize the ideal.*

Everything, according to spiritual metaphysics, is first worked out in the unseen before it is manifested in the seen, it is in the ideal before it is realized in the real, it is in the spiritual before it shows forth in the material. The Realm of the Unseen is the Realm of Cause. The Realm of the Seen is the Realm of Effect. The nature of effect is always determined and conditioned by the nature of the cause.

The SOMEHOW of Christmas *rests on the amazing wonder of God's revelation to us. It recognizes that the revelation comes to people in a variety of different ways, and it is revealed under all sorts of circumstances. Do not worry if your pattern does not follow another's pattern!*

The touchstone of the validity of the experience is this: *You are filled with an inner knowing that what is happening is right for you and is fulfilling a certain prophecy in your life.*

When it happens you will realize that what has gone before and seemed mysterious and inexplicable, now takes on the form of hidden meaning, and you will, therefore, be more inclined to trust God's guidance in the days to come.

SOMEHOW in life thinking persons find a meaning and a mission for their place in the scheme of things. What was your *somehow* as you look back over your experiences? Or is it *something* still to come?

3.

Sometime

"For to you is born this day in the city of David a Savior, who is Christ the Lord." (Luke 2:11)

It is a metaphysical teaching that the term "city of David," while it can be interpreted literally, is descriptive of "man as the Temple of God in which Christ as Savior is born anew." It maintains that being "saved by Christ" means to truly discover ourselves in Him and Him in us.

Esoteric religion has long taught that as Adam signified the *involving* soul, and as the Messiah expressed the *evolving* soul, so David, the new condition of man, represents that person in whom the *cosmic* soul is manifested. Thus, the "city of David" is that life in which this spiritual evolvement happens. It happens in that "Sometime" when we feel the overpowering birth of God's love and grace. It is then that "Christ is born in us."

Today great emphasis is placed on this kind of teaching. Some call it the Baptism of the Holy Spirit. Evangelists call it conversion. Many religionists refer to it as being "born again" or being "newborn in Christ." Liberal churchmen and metaphysicians call it a heightened consciousness, cosmic consciousness, and so on.

We try to attach a name to the phenomenon of the changed life, but this is only because we feel a need for identifying it, but we all know that it cannot actually be named. It is a spiritual awareness, like love, like beauty, like ecstasy that suddenly senses eternal values in the day-by-day experiences of life. *He who sees God, sees God in all things.* At this point the SOMEWHERE, the SOMEHOW, and the SOMETIME are recognized as one. This, in a very real way, is the "holistic" meaning of Christmas.

To repeat: SOMEWHERE in life we come to the place of spiritual integration; SOMEHOW in life we find our place in the scheme of things; SOMETIME in life we realize that God is very near to us — is *in* us, in fact. Christmas is, or should be, such a time.

Scholars notwithstanding, let's not make the Advent period a time for theological dialectics and debate. It is all very well to be esoteric, metaphysical, and doctrinaire about religion when the point is winning scholastic honors. But the gift of Christmas, like love, often defies the wisdom of the wise and reveals itself to the lowly and the otherwise, including the legendary "other Wise Man" who reached the manger rather late because of certain acts of mercy along the way. Some say he had a special audience with the manger Child. Could be that when we were children we were often nearer to the true spirit of Christmas than we are today.

Which may be what Charles Dickens had in mind when, in his essay *A Christmas Tree* he confided, "I do come home at Christmas. We all do, or we all should. We all come home, or ought to come home for a short holiday—the longer the better—home from the great boarding school (of life), where we are forever working at our arithmetical slates, home to take a bit of time and take a rest." This could have been the prescription which, as he noted in his Dr. Marigold, is *"To be taken for life."*

For SOMEWHERE, SOMEHOW, SOMETIME we all find the wonder and beauty of our oneness with God as we walk with Him at Christmas time in simplicity of mind and gentleness of heart.

SOMEWHERE .. "And Joseph also went up from Galilee, from the city of Nazareth, to Judea, to the city of David, which is called Bethlehem . . . ."

SOMEHOW .... "And she gave birth to her firstborn son and wrapped him in swaddling clothes, and laid him in a manger, because there was no place for them in the inn."

SOMETIME .... "For to you is born this day in the city of David a Savior, who is Christ the Lord."

"God bless us everyone!"

Chapter Eight

What's New About Christmas

"WHAT'S NEW ABOUT CHRISTMAS?"

Its Innovative Touch

The newest thing about Christmas is that it never grows old. Its ideals, emphasizing motherhood, peace, joy, and goodwill, never change. Every generation, every year finds its message dramatically alive with modern meaning and challenge. The hope-and-dream of Christmas, ages old, is ever new.

Fashions change, so do lifestyles, morals, standards, and our sense of values. Even the weather pattern changes as years come and go, but Christmas is eternally the same. Forever young, forever enchanting. And that's what's new about it.

At Christmas time, the old songs, from *Adeste Fideles* to *Good King Wenceslaus*, are as bright and shining and twice as precious as the new and novel Christmas decorations. There is never a Christmas without *Silent Night* joining the hit parade and *Away in a Manger* making its way back into people's hearts.

Someone is always reminding us that the clang of cash registers is drowning out the sound of Christmas chimes and that a pre-Christmas rip-off is often the order of the day. But what's new about all this is that the deeper the awareness of all these things, the greater becomes our faith that God, by virtue of the paradox, is very much in His heaven and all's right with the world for those who see beyond the seen and who view life with an inner knowing. And to those who feel the true spirit of the birth of Christ, Christmas is perennially, omnipotently new.

We can go even further. Granted that ambitious merchandisers have done their best to change the dress of Christmas trees by spraying, painting, flaking, tinting, and aerosoling them into all sorts of shades and shapes, the sight of an evergreen alive and growing is now being greeted with new spiritual understanding. Gently illuminated and lovingly festooned, a living tree sets our mind a-thinking until our heart is reaching back to memory lane.

And even though some Santas may be security guards in disguise or hired helpers with an eye on shoplifters down the crowded aisles — behind their beards are hidden the deeper thoughts of how the sound of music and the touch of children's hands give pause for the true meaning of Christmas.

What can be done about the secularization of Christmas? An innovative approach is to look at the phenomenon and see in it a *growing spiritualization of the secular in our world.* Consider images, for example. Once forbidden as all too worldly, they became such significant works of art that they immortalized every player in the cast of characters in the Bethlehem drama. *Secular* art, painting and sculpture, became *spiritualized.*

Music, ruled out of bounds by early Christian sects because of its worldliness, was so spiritualized by master composers that Christmas would hardly be Christmas without their contributions. The giving of gifts, condemned by many Christians because of the "infidelism" of the Zoroastrian Magi, has become the very heart of the Yuletide observances.

Give God time and the Spirit of Christmas half a chance, and what is now often labeled secularism will be recognized, because of the gift and the giver, as worthy of being a partner in a new and adventurous understanding of one's private, intimate relationship with God. Consider how satellites, carrying Christmas messages around the globe or exploring outer space, have caused us to increase our interest and wonder in the Bethlehem Star and seek its deeper meaning. Are these signs and wonders secular or spiritual? Or how about the affection for a pet, or a heart full of nostalgic memories, or a special moment of love on Christmas Eve? Be innovative. Spiritualize the secular.

Its Ecumenicity

Another thing that's new and interesting about Christmas is the fact that in days of old there was great concern on the part of the church-at-large to sort out what was Christian and what was pagan in the Advent observances. Great stress was put on the fact that December 25 should have nothing to do with the ancient celebration of a festival known as Brumalia (brumal meaning winter) which once observed the coming of the winter solstice. Church-goers were also warned that the Advent season should not be tainted by references to the Saturnalia, the ancient Roman festival that honored Saturn and heralded the rebirth of nature.

The Christmas tree, mistletoe, the giving of gifts, Santa Claus, the Yule log, all were under careful theological scrutiny and usually taboo to make certain there were no underground connections with fertility cults, gods, and goddesses.

Today, a new significance is being felt. The parallelisms of Christmas and the pre-Christian quest of humankind are being recognized, appreciated, and spiritually understood. Christ no longer needs any defense, apologist, or militant crusader. He can stand upon His own, and when He is lifted up, He lifts up all humankind. God today is recognized as ONE GOD, a god of both nature and humanity, a Sovereign not only of a "church" but of the Cosmos. In and through this spirit of understanding, all life and all human aspirations have become more hallowed and more personalized.

Today, clearer than ever before, we see in the birth of Christ the new birth of the Christ-consciousness within ourselves.

Christmas is now not only all-Christian, it is all-Spiritual, with a new challenge for individual growth, for all people everywhere. And since there is this newness about the meaning of Christmas for the individual, there is an equally significant meaning for every race, creed, and culture of the world. This "something new" is apparent to all who travel the jet-connected countries of the globe during the Christmas season.

Christmas stamps, Christmas stories, Christmas gifts, and Christmas observances are found in most major nations of the world. This does not mean that non-Christians are suddenly being converted to Christianity or that Christ is being accepted internationally as "Savior" in a Christian sense.

What it does mean is that there is a quietly growing, ever increasing awareness that the birth of Jesus represents a peak event in human experience, a focal point in history, and a giant forward step in humanity's march toward the ideals and philosophy which this "Prince of Peace" has come to represent.

Further evidence of this is found in the willingness on the part of the non-Christian world to recognize the moral and ethical principles proclaimed by Jesus.

The living religions of the world, no less than political leaders and statesmen, are re-examining and re-evaluating His life and mission. They are reviewing His approach to life,

His mystical touch in a practical world, His parables in the light of their intrinsic power, and the reach of His character and His charisma as He lived and died in support of His ideas.

In this respect Christmas has become universal, and the manger looms ever larger as an ecumenical shrine and symbol to be shared by people everywhere.

The Personal Imperative

By all odds, the newest thing about Christmas is YOU. Here you are a year older than last Christmas — or, are you a year younger because of all you have learned? It is a time for an inventory in the glowing light of Christmas faith — body, mind, spirit. One of the truest signs of youth is to find joy in Christmas. One of the surest evidences of aging is to get "Scroogey" roundabout this time of year!

Here you are with a year of remembrances, some good, some seemingly "un-good," some you never dreamed would happen, others that turned out just as you had planned. Life is full of changes, and Christmas comes again with its newness and freshness to remind us that every year must be taken in stride. If there is anything truly new about YOU at this time of the year, it is a conviction that the Christmas-in-you is a result of a mental perception, a spiritual conviction, a physical demonstration! Believe it! Live it!

But, you may say, here we are in an era of great uncertainty, an age of such completely unpredictable proportions that every Christmas price tag makes me check my Christmas list and recheck my credit cards.

Here we are in an exploding universe of four-plus billion people, and I am lost in the shuffle. Here we are, with many of my old landmarks, habits, customs, traditions, and convictions up for grabs. Here we are in a world that is becoming ever more impersonal, ever more high tech, more robotized, more materialistic, fatalistic, and dehumanized.

Yes, BUT.....here we are with Christmas in the air and, if you really listen, something will tell you that underneath your wrappings of caution and concern, a new person is being born in YOU, in ME, in EVERYONE who follows the Star and learns who and what we truly ARE!

That's the challenge and that's what's NEW!

A Summation

Christmas emphasizes a new and modern personalized faith. It speaks to each one of us individually, challenging us to have a personal confrontation with our highest good.

It reminds us that the Christ did not come to save the world en masse. His advent, His words, His acts, His philosophy were on the personal level. A new world evolves as individuals recognize their own potential God-likeness.

While this Man of Nazareth has often seemed to divide the world into various sects, opinions, denominations and beliefs, the experiencing of Him is the one unifying force among those who sincerely follow the Christian way. Christmas emphasizes this fact.

He is also bringing "non-Christians" into His fellowship through the growing interest and spiritual understanding of the Cosmic Christ. Surely it seems like a divine conspiracy —

a most intriguing one — on God's part to make this unforgettable Bethlehem figure all things to all men!

Ever and again the question and the learning about the
newness of Christmas prompt the unavoidably personal and
interestingly direct challenge, "What are you doing with what
He means to *you?*

You have heard the words before, but they must be
listened to again during this Christmastide, as phrased by
the Protestant eclectic, Dr. Albert Schweitzer, when he said:

> "He comes to us as one unknown, without a name, as of
> old, by the lakeside, He came to those who knew Him
> not. He speaks to us the same word, 'Follow me!' and
> sets us to tasks which He has to do in our time. He
> commands, and to those who obey Him, He will reveal
> Himself and we shall all learn in our own experience
> who He is."

And we must listen anew to a conclusion voiced by the
Catholic ecumenist Teilhard de Chardin when he
announced in his *Phenomenon-of-Man*:

> "To live and develop the Christian outlook needs an
> atmosphere of greatness and of connecting links. The
> bigger the world becomes and the more organic
> becomes its internal connections, the more will the
> perspectives of the Incarnation triumph. That is what
> believers are beginning, much to their surprise, to find
> out. Though frightened for a moment by evolution, the

Christian now perceives that what it offers him is nothing but a magnificent means of feeling more at one with God and of giving himself more to him.

"...at the present moment Christianity is the *unique* current of thought, on the entire surface of the noosphere, which is sufficiently audacious and sufficiently progressive to lay hold of the world, at the level of effectual practice, in an embrace, at once already complete, yet capable of indefinite perfection, where faith and hope reach their fulfillment in love. *Alone*, unconditionally alone, in the world today, Christianity shows itself able to reconcile, in a single living act, the All and the Person. Alone, it can bend our hearts not only to the service of that tremendous movement of the world which bears us along, but beyond, to embrace that movement in love."

So.............

"God rest you merry, gentlemen,
Let nothing you dismay,
Remember Christ, our Savior
Was born on Christmas Day!"

And so it is!

Chapter Nine

When Adonaiah Oakie Saw the Star

WHEN ADONAIAH OAKIE SAW THE STAR

A Parable

1.

Adonaiah Oakie was known as Old Scrooge. Especially at Christmas time. And most of all by the townsfolk of Middlebrook, Wisconsin, where he had lived his eighty years and built his home out of lumber from his own big mill. Adonaiah was rich. His house was large, and so was the pine tree in his front yard.

At Christmas time the townsfolk said, "For an outdoor Christmas tree the pine is a natural, but you'd never catch Old Scrooge putting as much as a light bulb on it."

And because the town somewhat had it in for Adonaiah, Adonaiah had it in for the town.

Adonaiah lived alone in the eleven-room house. His wife had died childless nearly thirty years ago. Since then he had sold the mill and become more and more of a recluse. Life, for Adonaiah, had become something of a stand-off. He wasn't one to socialize, and he wasn't one to travel.

"Say, Joe," the storekeeper said to the postmaster, "can you remember any good deed Old Scrooge ever did for anyone?"

"No, I sure can't."

Adonaiah didn't go to church. The minister once complained to the president of the church board, "Adonaiah Oakie simply hasn't any feeling for his fellowman, much less for the Lord."

The wife of the town banker told the mayor's wife, "Adonaiah Oakie ought to rent out part of his house to some young couple. It would do him a world of good to have someone around."

At a meeting of the town council where the members waiting for a quorum to show up, one of the members said, "You think we might interest Old Scrooge in a donation for the new park?"

"Adonaiah wouldn't put up a bird house if the wrens were singing at his window," was the reply.

Now it was Christmas, and Adonaiah wondered whether he ought to get a few presents for some of the folks in Middlebrook. He thought about this every year. Often when he got into bed as he did this time on the evening of December 20th, he lay for a long while looking up into the quivering moonlight as it filtered into his room through the branches of the big pine tree. He stretched his lean body and sighed. He really wanted to let his better self take over at this holy time of the year, but something said to him, "Let them first be decent to you. Don't you give in and have them say that Old Scrooge had to break down after all. You let them come around to you!" If there were only some way to be kind without being considered soft. If there were only some way to save face.

On this evening of December 20th when Adonaiah thought about "saving face," he thoughtfully stroked a hand over his lean and sagging cheeks. *His* face was getting older year by year. Some wrinkles were so deep he could put a finger in them. His hair was growing ever whiter, and thinner on top. His eyes — well, he would have to get his glasses changed again next time he went to the city. Something said, "If you're going to save face, Adonaiah, you'd better hurry or your old face won't be worth saving!" Then clear as a whisper came the inner warning, "Let them first be decent to you!" He nodded agreement and went to sleep.

The big house was very silent when, a short time later, Adonaiah opened his eyes. For a moment he lay there, not quite realizing where he was. This was unusual, considering that he knew every crook and corner of the room no matter what the hour. Then he saw the moonlight and the restless shadows.

He sat straight up in bed, listening. He thought he heard singing. He stayed very still and then decided it was his imagination. "You're not given much to dreaming, Adonaiah," he told himself, and that was true.

So he got up and went to the window. His squinting eyes searched the dark and then, suddenly, his glance caught something bright and shining in the big pine tree. It was a star. It hovered at the very peak of the old landmark. Adonaiah blinked at what he saw, suspiciously at first, then with wonder mingled with fear. His hands sought the window frame, and he stood there in his loose-fitting gray nightgown, a lanky, ghost-like figure shivering from cold and fright.

Getting hold of himself, he switched on the light and resolutely put on his glasses. Back to the window he went and gazed at the tip of the tree through his bifocals, from this angle and that, from down on his knees and up on his toes, from right and left. It was a star, there was no doubt about that. It was an honest-to-goodness star beaming in the moonlight on the big pine in his front yard.

"Adonaiah, you're dreaming," he told himself stubbornly and swung around to look angrily at the bed. He wouldn't have been surprised to have seen himself lying there, as if this were all a dream.

He took note of the room and all his old familiar things, from the fumed oak chest of drawers to the mahogany what-not which he had left just as his wife had wanted it, with the trinkets and the antique pieces as she had put them there long years ago.

He glanced at the two oval pictures on the wall, his father and mother. Anxiously he confronted the built-in wall safe, and his gaze rested for a moment on the combination lock. He shook himself to make sure he was awake, went to the mirror and reprimanded himself while looking sadly at his lean and wrinkled face. Stubbornly he switched off the light. Then he switched it on. Off and on, off and on — off. Back he went to the window. Trembling and cold, he stood there. The star twinkled and danced, so bright he took off his glasses and thoughtfully rubbed his eyes. Quietly he stood there, thinking and watching, while something said, "And there were shepherds in the fields, keeping watch over their flocks — and there came wise men from the East...."

Memory like a shining light went back across Adonaiah's years and showed up many half-forgotten things. The pictures in the oval frames were speaking. The trinkets on the what-not confided secrets to him. He seemed to hear the sound of the big saws of his father's mill as they cut through the long logs, and their sound was like voices trying to be heard. He was a boy going to school. A young man getting married. An old man growing weary of the town and its people. He saw life in all the thousands of things that go through people's mind at Christmas time.

But it dawned upon Adonaiah that this miracle of the star, or whatever it was, did not happen to every man. Was any other tree in Middlebrook so honored? Certainly not. Straining his tired eyes hard as he might, he could not see another hint of light on any tree in any other lawn anywhere. Something said to him, "Neither the storekeeper nor the banker nor anyone is having this experience. You can put it down that not even the members of the town board or the minister himself has a magic star shining in his yard. I tell you, Adonaiah, it was put there just for you!"

"Who put it there?" Adonaiah asked aloud.

There was no answer But what Adonaiah thought was this: If the good Lord put it there, He had surely made the first move. The Lord didn't say, "Let Adonaiah come to me first. *I've* got to save face. I don't want all the angels in heaven thinking that I am soft." No. The good Lord must simply have buried His pride this Christmas and said, "I'm going down and make up with Adonaiah Oakie. It's high time he and I got together. We're both getting older, and somebody ought to make the first move. And, after all, it's that time of year."

Adonaiah pressed his nose against the cold window and closed his eyes.

"Dear Lord," he prayed, "help me to be a little more like You."

When he opened his eyes, the star was moving. It was edging upward. Quickly Adonaiah searched for his glasses, but by the time he found them, the star was gone. More correctly, it was going. Like a silver shadow it was rising above the tall pine tree and drifting away into the night.

"Stay!" Adonaiah cried. "Stay until morning!"

But then he said in his heart, "No. Go your way. Go to the storekeeper and the banker and the postmaster and the members of the town board, go to all of them and let them see you, too. But tell them you were *here* first!"

2.

Bright and early in the morning, Adonaiah walked round-and-round the big tree. He looked at it wonderingly from every side. With and without his spectacles he gazed studiously at the topmost branches and at the spire that pointed upward straight as an arrow.

"Good morning, Adonaiah!" The mayor was on his way to his office. His greeting was a matter of course, and he kept on walking as he usually did, knowing that Old Scrooge would answer him with only a grunt. Then he stopped dead in his tracks.

"Good morning, Mr. Mayor!" came a reply. "Merry Christmas!"

"Why, yes," the major managed to say, "it is that time of the year."

"Stop in a moment, can you?" Adonaiah invited. "I was just sizing up the old tree. It would look real good with lights and a bit of decorating, don't you think? Say, maybe, with a star on top?"

"Oh, by all means!" the astonished mayor replied.

Adonaiah's tone was cautious, "You never saw a star atop here, did you?"

"I sure never did," said the mayor. "Neither has anyone else. Stars don't appear on trees by themselves, you know."

"Oh, don't they?" Adonaiah challenged, but quickly concealed his feelings. "Of course, you are right. You are absolutely right. Let's forget we said anything about a star." Then he was suddenly carried away by an uncontrollable impulse. "But this year," he heard himself boasting, "the old tree is going to have lights from tip to toe and gifts on every branch, and you can tell the boys and girls of Middlebrook they're going to see a Christmas like they never saw before!"

3.

When the mayor swung open his office door a few minutes later, he was out of breath.

"My heavens!" he exclaimed. "The day of miracles certainly isn't past. Adonaiah Oakie is decorating the big tree and staging a community Christmas for all the kids in town!"

"Run that past me again?" said the town clerk.

"What happened to the old geezer?" the town treasurer wanted to know.

"He wouldn't say," said the mayor. "Get me the school superintendent on the phone."

The superintendent told the minister and the minister told the members of his church board and they told the storekeeper and the postmaster, and by mid-morning the news was all over town. People talked about it on the streets and in their homes, and the editor of the Middlebrook *New*

Era set up a front page story: GIGANTIC CHRISTMAS PARTY PLANNED ON OAKIE ESTATE. *Adonaiah Oakie, one of Middlebrook's most respected citizens, told the New Era today that a Christmas party is scheduled for the afternoon of December 24th. All children and young people of Middlebrook and vicinity are INVITED. The landmark pine on the lawn of the estate will be appropriately decorated, and the lights will be turned on at six o'clock when the mayor pulls the switch...."*

By mid-afternoon the villagers were telephoning Adonaiah how wonderful they thought it all was, and the following day groups of youngsters were gathering around the tree to watch the crews of workmen preparing for the celebration.

Expectation rose to such a pitch that by the day before Christmas it was necessary for the town marshal to play the role of security guard for the first time in Middlebrook's history. The bank locked its doors at noon. The stores closed early. Even the post office, though it was contrary to regulations, clamped down the stamp window and stuck up a sign: "Gone to Adonaiah Oakie's Christmas Party!"

The day was made to order. A gentle morning snowfall laid a white skirt on Middlebook streets and gave the big tree a touch which the decorators could never have achieved. It made the white-winged angel figures even whiter and caused the multi-colored crystal balls to glow like prisms. The *New Era* photographer, who had taken pictures of the town for over forty years, admitted there had never been a scene like this. He had his camera set up in the window of

131

Adonaiah's bedroom for the difficult shot of the unforgetta-ble moment when the mayor pulled the switch on the tree's encircling strands of lights.

Adonaiah had never known such a day. He felt as if the spirit of Christmas depended upon him and, as far as he was concerned, the Holy Night was being touched off all over the world by what was happening in his front yard.

"Ladies and Gentlemen!" announced the minister. "Your attention, please! The children will now sing *O—Little—Town—of—Bethlehem.* During the second verse the light will be turned on by His Honor, the Mayor of Middlebrook!"

And on this cue, a hundred Middlebrook children lifted their hearts in song.

Tears stood in Adonaiah's eyes, and the lights that sud-denly sprang to life on the big tree were like a burst of glory. As the awed cheers of the crowd swept over him, he was lost in wonder and joy, wishing that life could always be the way it was this moment when, for a little while, the spirits of many people were merged into one, and he was in the center of it all.

This was by no means the climax. Suddenly Santa Claus strode from the big house, his bulging red and white attire covered with a string of copper sleigh bells, the very ones that Adonaiah's father once used on the black team in the olden days when the lumber mill was running high.

When Santa began distributing the gifts of candies, balloons, and little boxes full of animal cut-out Christmas cookies, someone struck up a song. It was the storekeeper, and he was setting the tune for "He's a jolly good fellow!" No one had any doubt for whom the words were intended. Even Santa Claus took off his red-tasseled cap and made a grand gesture in the direction of Adonaiah Oakie.

And because the town loved Adonaiah, Adonaiah loved the town.

He wandered among the groups of children as they unwrapped their gifts. He heard their excited exclamations as they chorused, "Gee, thank you, Mr. Oakie!" At one point, a youngster of twelve came to him.

"Mr. Oakie," said the boy, "my mother said to tell you that my grandfather and your father were good friends."

"Of course," Adonaiah agreed. "You're the Eddington boy, aren't you?"

"Joseph," was the reply. "My mother said that one Christmas long ago *your* father gave *my grandfather* lumber from the mill so he could build back his house that had burned down. It was in that new house that *my* father was born, and *I* was born there, too."

"Well, well," murmured Adonaiah.

"So you see, Mr. Oakie, if *your* father hadn't done that for *my grandfather*, I might not even have been born!"

"Now that is some figuring," said Adonaiah.

"You have never ever been in our house, have you?" Joseph asked.

"No."

"If you come, I'll show you my airplane. I'll even let you fly it. It's this long. Two feet. You just set it for flying, and off it goes."

"Someday I must see it."

"Or some *night*," said Joseph. "You ought to see it at night. It shines just like a star."

"Well, well," murmured Adonaiah and, patting the boy gently on the shoulder, he moved on.

Yes, that was true about the lumber all right. His father had freely given the Eddingtons every single piece they needed. Adonaiah hadn't thought of that for a long time, but he was happy that the deed was well remembered. He would have to go over to the Eddingtons sometime and see the house from the inside. He would even like to see Joseph's airplane. The one with the wing spread "this long." The one that "shines like a star."

The words pulled Adonaiah to an abrupt stop. His body stiffened. "Shines like a star!" he said half-aloud. He raised his eyes to the top of the big pine where a white bulb burned brilliantly on the topmost spire and where the white snow sparkled. He whirled around and glowered back to where Joseph and the group of boys were huddled. Determinedly he started over to them, but they were so busy talking they never saw him even though he stopped not three feet away. They, too, were looking at the tree. One boy, shielding his eyes as he looked to the very top, was asking, "But wasn't it hard climbing way up there in the dark, Joseph?"

"Not bad," Joseph boasted. "The airplane wasn't stuck very tight. All it needed was a push, and off it went!"

"Weren't you scared?"

"I climb a lot," said Joseph.

"Scared of Old Scrooge, I mean," the boy exclaimed. "What if he'd caught you?"

"I was scared of that," Joseph admitted. "But I wouldn't be anymore. He's for real!"

"Sure he is," was the response. "We'd never ought to call him Old Scrooge again."

"Nobody better call him that if I'm around!" Joseph vowed, flexing his arms and biting off the head of an animal cracker.

"That goes for me, too!"

"And for me!"

"And me!"

As Adonaiah heard this, he tiptoed away. His consternation left him. He shook his head in wonder as he contemplated the topmost branches of the old tree. The next moment he was chuckling to himself so merrily that a great wave of good feeling fell over all who heard him.

"Hold it, Adonaiah!" called the photographer. "That's the picture of you I want, laughing just like that! It *is* a great event, isn't it?"

"You'll never know the half of it," said Adonaiah. "Where do you want me to stand?"

"You're great right where you are!"

The picture, run by the *New Era* on its front page, showed Adonaiah Oakie standing within reach of the big pine tree. It showed the lights and the decorations and the snow-white branches, and some folks in Middlebrook still say that if you could look high enough, you could also see a star shining brightly at the very top.

Chapter Ten

Of Mother and Child

OF MOTHER AND CHILD

1.

Inspiration and the Miraculous

The story of Christmas rightly assumes that we mortals believe in miracles. The annunciation, the angels' song, the guiding star, the fulfillment of prophecy are presented in the New Testament not simply as facts, but as gospel truth. And so it is with the major miracle of all: the virgin birth of a child in a manger, destined to be known and worshipped around the world.

Well and good. Life is alive with the unexplained and the phenomenal. Birth is always a miracle, and at the heart of the Christmas legend is the sanctification of motherhood everywhere, no less than a universal adoration of mother and child.

Luke, the physician, reported the event of the birth in Bethlehem simply and graphically:

"And she gave birth to her firstborn son and wrapped him in swaddling clothes, and laid him in a manger, because there was no place for them in the inn." (Luke 2:7)

Medieval artists, among them Leonardo da Vinci, immortalized Mary and her firstborn in a series of masterworks. Renaissance sculptors, few greater than Luca della Robbia, created tabernacles for their versions of the Nativity.

Classical composers, such as Johann Sebastian Bach, composed words and music for immortal Christmas oratorios, including the majestic chorales honoring "Madonna and Child":

"Break forth, O beauteous heavenly light,
And usher in the morning,
Ye Shepherds, shrink not with affright,
But hear the angels' warning:
This Child, how weak in infancy,
Our confidence and joy shall be,
The power of Satan breaking,
Our peace eternal making."

American poets, James Russell Lowell, for one, made the event part and parcel of Christian hymnody:

"What means this glory round our feet,
The Magi mused, more bright than morn?
And voices chanted clear and sweet,
Today the Prince of Peace is born!"

Appalachian folklore included the Bethlehem miracle in our country's spirituals:

"When Mary birthed Jesus 'twas in a cow's stall
With wise men and farmers and shepherds and all,
But high from the heavens a star's light did fall,
And the promise of ages it then did recall.

"I wonder as I wander out under the sky,
How Jesus the Savior did come for to die.
For poor ornery mortals like you and like I."

2.

Mother and Child

During our travel assignments it dawned on me that we were being exposed to another impressive portrayal of the romantic tradition of mother and child, and in a most contemporary setting.

The awareness began some twelve years ago when Lorena and I returned from a research trip in Southeast Asia. As photographer in our intercultural junkets, she does a great deal of freelancing on her own. Nature scenes, animal life, remote places of worship, people off the beaten path, are all part of the documentary job.

Invariably she returned from these trips with "mother and child" pictures that seemed to me not only basic to our relationship with life in the countries and cultures visited, but the photos were also strikingly reminiscent and reflective of the Christmas miracle as represented by artists, poets, musicians, no less than folklore and tradition.

Ladakh

There was, for example, this thought-provoking portrait taken in Ladakh, a remote and rarely visited region at the northwestern end of the Himalayas in the State of Kashmir. Here, some 12,000 feet above the gaping valley where the Indus River flows, a village woman was on her way to market.

How long had mothers in this inaccessible land lived their lives, unnoticed and unknown, themselves as unaware of us in the "outside" world as we were of them?

History in Ladakh dates back to the beginning of the Christian Era when its religion was Buddhism and its monasteries centers of Tibetan mystical rites. In 400 A.D. it was visited by a lone Chinese pilgrim on a spiritual quest. In the twelfth century, having become aware of the strategic lay of the land, Moslem invaders overran the country. Today Ladakh, absorbed by India, is a country half Buddhist and half Moslem with only minor inroads made by Christian missionary work. The photograph of "Mother and Child" retold the unforgettable story of the changelessness of love and life in a changing world.

Gabon

Dignity, beauty, and grace were so evident in this African mother and child that the picture remains a coveted remembrance of a strenuous trip to Dr. Albert Schweitzer's medical encampment in Lambarene, located in what at the time was known as French Equitorial Africa. By good fortune our Polaroid camera provided this woman with her first portrait of herself. We titled the photograph "Melons to Market", but more correctly it is a graphic symbol of the universal durability and power of motherhood about which we men have known all too little, all too long.

Morocco

Two thousand miles northwest of Lambarene, across the vast reaches of the African continent, another woman was going to market during Lorena's photographic *jornada* to Morocco. On the long and lonely road to Marrakech this Islamic mother willingly paused for a moment in the camera's eye. Wearing the traditional Moslem veil, proud of the baby at her side, she fit into the Christmas story in a most remarkable way.

Mexico

So did this Mexican mother and child photographed a year later astride their burro on the road to Chalma.

The Christmas connection with donkeys and burros becomes apparent when we read the Bethlehem story in its entirety, beyond the coming of the Magi with their gifts.

". . . behold, an angel of the Lord appeared to Joseph in a dream and said, 'Rise, take the child and his mother, and flee to Egypt, and remain there till I tell you; for Herod is about to search for the child, to destroy him'." (Mathhew 2:13)

How *did* Mary and Joseph travel the estimated hundred and more miles from Nazareth to Egypt? Two thousand years ago the vehicles of the time were camels, and there is no record that the Wise Men left any of their steeds in the manger along with their gifts of gold, frankincense, and myrrh!

Most researchers contend that the Holy Family trudged on foot and by donkey over byways and uncharted parts thereby avoiding the risk of capture by Herod's men. However it was accomplished, a hint of primitive travel was graphically suggested by our photographs in foreign lands, particularly that of the Islamic mother and child in Marrakech, and the Catholic *madre* with her firstborn on a lonely road in Mexico.

We Christians rightly tend to believe that faith, as a factor in parental love, is strengthened by the Nativity of Christ and the "keeping of Christmas." It is unfair, however, to confine this assumption merely to the one billion avowed believers in the world of Christendom. The love of mother for child is universal, equally deep in all cultures and correspondingly instinctive in Christian and non-Christian mothers alike.

Japan

Studying this unposed photoprint (the original is in color), who can fail to catch the mystique in the mother's glance or the profoundness of her affection!

This is a mother and child of the Shinto faith, photographed at a religious festival in Osaka, an observance that combined not only principles of Shintoism, but of Buddhism and Christianity as well.

Bhutan

Come and meet this young Bhutanese mother and child who we came upon in Thimpu during a Buddhist festival in this legendary Himalayan country. When Lorena impulsively greeted the mother with, "Please don't move!," the young woman clasped the child closer, protectively. Language was more of a barrier than a line of communication, but Lorena's appeal proved persuasive.

Bhutan, once part of Tibet, had been closed to tourism and the outside world until 1974. Heartland of the "Thunder Dragon" people, who once believed that thunder in the mountains was evidence of a fearsome dragon, it was a country which until the mid-twentieth century had never seen a wheel. Now a mini-monarchy in a spectacular, awe-inspiring land of mountains, fields, and foothills, it had opened itself to the modern world — note the woman's wristwatch and bobby pin!

But Bhutan held other significant interest — the quiet mood of the people, the cattle stalls beneath many of the houses, the setting, and the sentiment gave us an imaginative perspective of the way life might have been in the era when Jesus was born.

Guatemala

With a dignity worthy of the Holy Mother, this Guatema-
lan madonna and child emerged from a market in Chichi-
castenango. The overhanging arch suggested an artist's
touch honoring the *Sancta Virg Virginum* (Holy Virgin of
Virgins).

Poland

Political and ideological lines may differ, customs may be dissimilar, but nothing is more certain than the universal ties between mother and child. Motherhood is, after all, beyond the divisive principles formulated and instituted by man. Here in Poland, where Latin Christianity persists within the framework of a relentless communist government, a "madonna and child" happily consented to a cherished *Weselych Swiat* (Merry Christmas) portrait and a fond remembrance of a lovely interchange of fellowship.

Ecuador

Sentiment has its way of playing games. When Lorena came to me with this dramatic portrait of an Indian mother taken on a lonely road in the highlands of Ecuador, I asked myself, "Could these penetrating eyes, this face filled with pathos, challenge and spirit, have been more like the face of Mary than the docile Madonnas and hallowed Virgin Mothers reverently depicted by romanticists?"

What was she truly like, this woman who gave birth to the Prince of Peace?

Influenced by artists, inspired by sculptors, conditioned in our thinking by poets, hymnists, legends and folklore, we still maintain the liberty of creating the Holy Family in our own image and imagination.

United States of America

In our Western world, particularly in the U.S.A. with its many freedoms and everchanging mores, the role of mother and child would require a portfolio all its own. The most popular qualities about our relationships and innovations, the most photographic expressions, are laughter and joy. Particularly at Christmas, the picture-taking mood is always festive. We want everyone to *"smile and be happy.! "*

We happened to be in Zion National Park in Utah shortly before it closed for the winter and holiday season. Here in the enchanted canyon, carved by the Virgin River, the giant monolithic walls and prehistoric evidences of life (fossils) dating back more than 200,000,000 years, persuaded us to stand in silent thought.

By chance, as we were making our way to what is called "The Great White Throne," we met a typical young American mother with her first-born child strapped to a cradle-board, Indian-style. Here was a serendipitous scene of merriment and oneness with life.

Surely there must have been occasions when Mary laughed, and the infant Jesus, too, though most Christians consistently identify Him in His adult years as "a man of sorrows and acquainted with grief."

Christmas puts it all together: the miracle and the mystery, the power and the glory, the wish and will to believe.

Advent is a time for taking inventory of what Christmas really means to us. Each year, as we relive the spirit of the coming of the Prince of Peace, the challenge of it deepens, the religions built upon the historic fact of it are asked to reassess their honest convictions and their goals. And, as a special gift, we are given the privilege to reflect within ourselves and to respect in others, Christian and non-Christian alike, the greatest story every told of the wondrous love and the spiritual essence in the relationship of MOTHER AND CHILD.

Chapter Eleven

Christmas in Other Lands

CHRISTMAS IN OTHER LANDS

Mexico

If there is ever a time I wish I were two people, it is at Christmas. I want to be at home where we keep the day according to our traditions, and I want to be traveling to see how Christmas is kept around the world.

I can trace this feeling to the time several years ago when I was waiting for car repairs in Mexico two days before Christmas. There was no chance to get home, and I imagined that a small-town hotel would be a place devoid of Yuletide cheer.

"What's going on in the way of Christmas?" I asked the clerk behind the cramped-in desk.

"*Posadas*," he said. "Ever see a *posada*?"

"Don't I have to get into a home for something like that? Wouldn't I need to know someone here?"

157

"Every house is a home at Christmas," he replied, and that is how I became for one evening a villager in the little town of San Miguel.

I walked in a procession of some forty chanting worshippers, led by two children carrying a small litter which held the figures of Joseph and Mary seated on a burro. Each of us carried a lighted candle as we strolled through the crisp, enchanted night. We approached a small house, an adobe home, and I could not help but think that this must have been the kind of place found in the land where Christmas was born, a home that God and man had built together out of the stuff of the earth.

One of the men in the procession rapped at the door.

"Who's there?" asked a gruff voice inside.

"Mary and Joseph. They want lodging for the night."

"There is no room."

"They have traveled far. All the way from Nazareth."

"There is no room."

"Mary is expecting a child. A child is to be born."

A stillness hung over our little world. Even the children who had tried to entertain me with their antics were silent. The women, wrapped in their *rebozos*, the men in their *serapes*, were like a group which might actually have clustered around the Bethlehem stable long years ago.

The adobe door opened, and the householder said, "Come in. There is a corner here you can have. There is straw here for Joseph and Mary."

The figures were set down in the straw where a *nacimiento*, a manger scene, had been prepared. We knelt for an "*Ave Maria*" and an "Our Father." Then a chant was intoned:

"O gracious pilgrim,
O purest Mary,
I offer thee my soul
To be thy refuge."

Posada means "lodging." Legend says that Mary and Joseph had to beg lodging eight nights during their journey from Nazareth to Bethlehem. On the ninth night, Christmas Eve, the figure of the Christ Child was placed in the *nacimiento*.

Now the serious mood was broken by a youngster's shout: "*Pinata!* " He pointed to a large clay pot suspended from the ceiling. This was the *pinata*, lavishly decorated with crepe paper and filled with gifts.

One by one the children were blindfolded, given a *palo* (broomstick), and spun around until they were dizzy. Then they tried to smash the *pinata*. Each had three tries at it, but their blows went wild, especially since the *pinata* was on a rope, and a man kept maneuvering it up and down and out of reach.

After the children, it was my turn. Blindfolded and dizzy, I would have had no better luck than the others, only that I suspect the leader placed the *pinata* directly in my line of attack. My *palo* connected with the clay pot, and down came a shower of shards, small boxes, trinkets, and candy. During the mad scramble to gather up as much as possible, an elderly Mexican woman picked up a tiny ribboned box. We waited expectantly as she walked about contemplating the box and then came to me, saying, "This is for our friend."

She placed the gift affectionately into my hands. I opened it and, to the delight of all of us, held up a rosary of white beads and a silvery cross.

Everywhere throughout Mexico and Latin American countries people had their *posadas* and the breaking of the *pinata*, but this experience was my first, and it drew me closer to the heart of a joyous and believing people.

"*Ustedes son mis amigos* . . . . you are my friends," I said, and the generous feeling of Christmas held us in its spell.

West Germany

During one Advent season, a writing assignment took me to Germany, a country traditionally rich in Yuletide lore. It was now a divided land: the East German Democratic Republic in the Soviet sector and the West German Federal Republic. The Soviet zone had built its wall dividing Berlin after some three million East Germans had emigrated. Parts of Berlin and numerous cities in the Federal Republic still showed the wounds and malice of war. Ruin and suffering were agonizingly widespread, but Christmas, the eternal star in man's darkest sky, was calling people to return to the Prince of Peace.

In West Germany's cities — Berlin, Munich, Hamburg, Essen — stores and streets were decorated. In the villages there was scarcely a home without a Christmas wreath or tree. Churches, many of them cold and only partially rebuilt, were filled with worshippers. In Frankfurt, children were flocking to the Opera House to see a performance of *Hansel and Gretel*. In Stuttgart, still crippled in war's aftermath, a huge illuminated tree stood in a swale of rubble, with a large sign: "Beyond the blackest night, the dawn is breaking." I delivered some American gift packages in a tenement house in Kassel and heard a phonograph playing *White Christmas*.

In Bocholt, where I was a guest in a refugee home, the family had its traditional *Advent-Kranz*, an evergreen wreath suspended horizontally from the ceiling by four ribbons. In the wreath were four white candles, one for each Advent Sunday.

The family was there, father, mother, two daughters, and a son. The lighting of candles can be a very simple thing. But when on this fourth and final Sunday of Advent my host said, "You must light the *Advent-Kranz*," it became for me a sacred ritual. First there was a prayer of thankfulness for peace. Then the father timed a Scripture text (John 8:12) to my lighting of the four tapers: "I am the LIGHT of the world; he who follows ME does not walk in darkness, but will have the LIGHT of LIFE." After this we joined hands around the wreath and sang the most famous of all Christmas hymns, *Stille Nacht, Heilige Nacht* (*Silent Night*). The song filled the room with a spirit that helped heal the scars and thoughts of war.

Russia

On Christmas day I went over into the Russian sector and on to Moscow. A hotel clerk in West Berlin cautioned me about the trip, but added, "At Christmastime you will not have the difficulty you might have at other times. The spirit of Christmas gets over the Russian line."

He was right. I encountered no special inconvenience. But the train trip and the walk from the East Berlin station to *Marien Kirche* added up to a long and lonely journey. This was at the height of the Stalin regime. Giant portraits of the dictator hung on the buildings, and huge signs said: "With hammer and sickle, with book and gun, forward into Socialism!"

The air was heavy as the leaden sky. No sound of carols, no laughter, no Christmas trees, no lighted candles were in evidence. But *Marien Kirche* was crowded to the doors, and no watchers forbade anyone to go in.

Some 800 people sat huddled in the unheated church, silent and resigned. They represented the older generation, and their devotion was unquestioned as they silently contemplated the *Krippe*, the large, simply fashioned Nativity scene. The minister came in and climbed into the high pulpit. Songs were sung, songs of the Christmastide which are never without hope and never without the hint of childlike faith. One must hear *Silent Night* in such a setting to understand how idealistic and how filled with the divine nature of things it truly is.

I attended two services. Later, on the way back to West Berlin a German woman sat facing me in the train. She was clutching a small Christmas parcel. Only after I convinced her that I was an American could I engage her in a German conversation. In a quiet whisper she confided, "I live in the Russian *zone*. I would be thankful if I lived here in the *sector*. Those in the sector wish they could live in *West Berlin*. Those in West Berlin would give much to live in *West Germany*. Those in West Germany would give even more to live in the *United States*."

Her eyes were full of longing, but when she got off at her destination, just before I crossed through the "Iron Curtain," she said with typically undying human hope, "*Froehliche Weinachten* . . . Merry Christmas to you!"

Christmas in Non-Christian Countries

Christmas in non-Christian countries can also be a rich experience. Invariably all of the world's great religions respect and appreciate the spirit of the Nativity and find in their own beliefs some relationship with the miracle of Bethlehem.

In Burma, Japan, and Ceylon the Buddhists feel they know what the deeper meaning of Christmas signifies: God revealing Himself anew to man. In Islamic Pakistan, I heard the Salvation Army sing carols and solicit help for the poor. "Christmas," said a Pakistani, "makes us all more charitable."

In India, where only three percent of the 750,000,000 inhabitants are Christian, I saw Parsees, Hindus, Moslems, and Sikhs distribute special gifts to the poor and the homeless.

On the island of Haiti which, of course, is officially Christian, I went one Christmas Eve into the Plaine de Leogane to witness a Christian-Voodoo ceremony. Here the Christmas narrative had penetrated primitive Voodoo beliefs. The counterpart of the Virgin Mary was a *loa* (a spiritual entity) known as Erzilie Freda. At midnight, Haitian mothers brought their babies to be baptized as a remembrance that on this mystical night a Sacred Child made all children more holy. To the beat of drums and the whir of Christian and Voodoo chants, the *loa* and the Christian Holy Family were blended and worshipped in their primitive and highly emotionalized ritual as if religion knew no barriers and Christmas no denominational bounds.

Bethlehem

But my most vivid recollection of Christmas away from home will always be the unforgettable country where Christ was born. Like anyone who from earliest childhood has been indoctrinated with the Christmas story, my goal was Bethlehem.

I went there years ago and have been there again of late. The miracle persists. The first time I was there was in the days of the Mandelbaum Gate. I saw the miracle of Christmas. I was permitted to walk through that narrow, barbed-wire corridor, where men with tommy-guns kept their uneasy and unbroken vigil. You did not easily pass to and fro across this "no man's land" at any time excepting Christmas and Easter. The miracle to me was when the guards on both sides of the Mandelbaum Gate put aside their guns and Arabs and Israelis waved to each other as if to indicate that all was well, that for forty-eight hours there would be no incidents. For this sublime and holy period, faith conquered fear. For a little while it stilled the unrest and quieted the suspicion between the Arab League countries and State of Israel. Today, at this writing, tensions still persist, but today the miracle also prevails.

Now the pilgrims come: Christians who live in Israel, Christians from all over the world, Christians of every denomination and color and station. Many are singing. Others pray audibly. Some pierce the sacred night with shouts of greeting to a relative or friend. Lanterns and torches vie with the searchlights on the military cars standing incongruously in a momentarily united Holy Land.

I will long remember the medley of languages as I walked with the crowds. But I will never forget the moments of silence when the spirit of the world is absorbed in the universal language of man's immortal hope. "On, on to Bethlehem!" was the unspoken word. By car, by burro, by bicycle, the crowds moved forward, but the true pilgrim will always go on foot. He will go first to the Shepherds' Field at the foot of Bethlehem town. He will find the night filled with music and the sky bright with stars.

The Magi, it is said, had to travel for six days, but the lowly shepherds were practically within sight of the manger when the angels broadcast the news. As I walked in the throng I imagined myself both Wise Man and shepherd walking where Joseph and Mary walked, the path leading to the "Inn" where there was no room and when the stable was made to do. The miracle has transformed the stable into the celestial

Church of the Nativity with a gateway so low you must kneel to enter it, and that is as it should be.

The crib has been glorified with marble and jewels, and on the spot where it is believed by many that Jesus was born, a solid gold star has been implanted. The stable, which was actually little more than a cave, has become a shrine, and the church is a most hallowed spot for Midnight Mass on Christmas Eve.

The Christian desire is usually to return to Bethlehem alone, without the crowds, without the singing and the prayers. To return, if it were possible, to walk by oneself — on some crisp and starry night — from the Shepherds' Field to the manger bed.

But as I think of this, I realize again how universal Christmas is and how it draws all people into its mystical spell, and I decide, unless fate wills it otherwise, I will spend Christmas at home around a gaily lighted, decorated tree which, as is our custom, will be placed near the big window in the front room. Beautifully wrapped gifts, Christmas cards, delicacies and music will transform the house into a fairyland dwelling. We will go to our church for the Christmas Eve program, then come home and open our gifts. And, as we often do, we will go to a Catholic Midnight Mass, because of Christmas.

Home for us is America, and Christmas in America, as we have seen, is many things. It is the Dutch carrying the Star of Bethlehem through the streets on a pole. It is the Swiss caroling from house to house, carrying a music box that tinkles out quaint Yuletide hymns. It is the Italians fashioning their *presepis*, their Nativity scenes. It is the Scots observing Twelfth Night with a Nativity play. It is the English enjoying their wassail bowl and their Yule log just as they do throughout the Commonwealth. It is the Scandinavians observing the feast day of St. Lucia, the Moravians burning their beeswax tapers, the Russians blessing the waters, the Spanish enacting *Los Pastores*. It is the French, the Czechs, the Irish, the Germans, the people of all nationalities singing their sacred hymns and keeping their Yuletide customs just as they did in their homeland.

Christmas in America! A montage of freedom's children, a unity of many nations, an everlasting belief that the Bethlehem Star still shines and that the angels' song still sounds its hope of "Peace on Earth, Good Will to Men!"

So, because of Christmas:

Schenorhavor Dzenount	(Armenian)
Vesele Vanoce	(Bohemian)
Chestita Koleda	(Bulgarian)
Kung Hsi Hsin Nien	(Chinese)
Stretan Bozic	(Croatian)
Vesele Vanoce	(Czechoslovakian)
Glaedelig Jul	(Danish)
Vroolijk Kerfeest	(Dutch)
Gajan Kristnaskon	(Esperanto)
Roomsaid Joulu Puhi	(Estonian)
Hauskaa Joulua	(Finnish)
Joyeux Noel	(French)
Froehliche Weihnachten	(German)
Kala Christougena	(Greek)
Mele Kali-ki-mahu	(Hawaiian)
Chag Ha-molad Sameach	(Hebrew)
Boldog Karacsomy	(Hungarian)
Nodlaig Nait Cugat	(Irish)

Because of Christmas

Buon Natale	(Italian)
Meri Kurisumasu	(Japanese)
Feliz Navidad	(Mexican)
Gledelig Jul	(Norwegian)
Weselych Swiat	(Polish)
Boas Festas	(Portuguese)
Sarbatori Vesele	(Rumanian)
S Roshestvom Khristovym	(Russian)
Felices Pascuas	(Spanish)
Glad Jul	(Swedish)
Srozhdestvom Kristovym	(Ukranian)
Nadolig Llawen	(Welsh)

And all together now, "MERRY CHRISTMAS TO ALL!"

Chapter Twelve

Of Christmas Time and Tide

OF CHRISTMAS TIME AND TIDE

A Fantasy

Never a Christmas without my favorite daily morning chore: winding up Old Seth. Throughout the year the job is routine, but on Christmas and New Years mornings the act is a ritual, for the dignified 9″ x 12″ clock — its rosewood case smooth as silk, its ticking strong and free, its hourly striking as sound as its bell — has been in our family for at least four generations, a Christmas gift. Tradition has it that it was handed down from a great-grandfather. Behind the smoothly swinging brass pendulum is an illegible date that could be 1830 or 1839. While the year is debatable, there is no question about the unfaded black-lettered printing that reads: SETH THOMAS, THOMASON, CONN. WARRANTED GOOD.

Warranted good, to be sure! The infallible ticking and the counting of the hours were intimately involved in my boyhood years. I remember Old Seth from the time the clock stood on the fireplace mantle in my parental home, too high for me to reach. My parents treasured it from the day of their marriage when it was handed down to them by an uncle of my mother's who remembered it from his youth, and so on, backward into time.

What intrigued me most about OLD SETH throughout the passing years was that this master product of New England's most famous clockmaker was never referred to as *it*. Old Seth was never neuter. We addressed and spoke of him as *he* as naturally as we did the Lord. "Have you wound him?" "What time does he say?" "I just heard him strike." "Who let him run down?" His personification was taken for granted, and his sex was Simon pure. No one was ever accused of being chauvinistic when they spoke of him as *him.*

There was another taken-for-granted familiarity about Old Seth. He had to be wound regularly because he was strictly a 30-hour clock. That was his circadian cycle. That was how his maker had made him and, if he ran down, there was no one to blame but the keeper of the key.

I cannot recall a single instance in all his years that he was ever ailing or complaining or under stress or that he needed therapy. The only special attention accorded him was my dad's self-appointed ceremony of placing a small pad of cotton dampened with a touch of kerosene inside the rosewood case just behind the pendulum. The gentle scent of this, my father claimed, was good for Seth's soul and quicked his spirit. The ceremony was performed twice a year, along about Easter and roundabout Christmas. This small courtesy and punctual winding were all Seth needed to keep on ticking and striking and faithfully fulfilling his mission in life.

We never had to worry about Old Seth the way we did about other timepieces. From the eccentric antique English grandfather's clock that stood on the stairs in my boyhood home, to the Swiss cuckoo clock outside the back door that stopped every time the faintest breeze brushed its wooden pendulum, to the electric clock that played dead whenever the power line conked out, all were temperamental. If any of these clocks weren't set or hung on a perfectly even keel, they would stop short as if never to go again. Not so with Seth. I promise you, if you tilted him a bit, he would defy gravity. You could move him off center, and he would tick as normally as if these little challenges were just what he needed to prove his worth. As far as his approach to life was concerned, Old Seth was always on the level.

I liked to feel that Seth and I had our private, special love affair. Though he had countless friends, his affection for me, I romanticized, went back to that long ago day when my father hoisted me up on a chair and showed me how to wind the two arbor gears that governed Old Seth's timing and striking functions. From that moment on, Seth and I had our secrets. On the occasion that I was permitted to tuck the kerosened wad of cotton under the swinging pendulum, our romance was quite complete.

Later on, for more than twenty summers, Old Seth reigned over the fireplace mantle in our log cabin on Kootenay Lake in British Columbia. He was also with Lorena and me in an apartment in Chicago during some tough and trying years. He shared an office with me on two university campuses in somewhat more prosperous days, and he was packed away in storage when our cultural assignments took us to Asia and the Middle East. I often thought about him during those arduous months, wondering how he recorded the unconscious passing of time and what haunting dreams he must be having in a Bekins bin. And now, as I write this with Christmas in mind, it is reassuring to have him here in our California home, within reach in my study, ticking away with the vigor of youth, his face serene with the wisdom of age, trusting me with all his heart that I will never let him run down or miss his semi-annual anointing with the holy oil of kerosene.

This brings me to a recall of a New Year's morning when, after celebrating overly much with friends and following the TV festivals of *Auld Lang Lyne* from Times Square to Hollywood, I entirely forgot for once in my life to wind Old Seth. When I overslept on New Year's morning and awoke with him on my mind, my intention was to go straight to his door. Inadvertently, however, I paused to turn on the TV because my subconscious was telling me that the Pasadena Rose Parade was already in full swing. One look at the sensational floats and fanfare got me hooked. For years I had been among those who camped out all night along the parade route, which beat bleacher viewing by a long shot and afforded a generous slice of modern Americana. Now here on my TV screen was the full force of what our high-tech, computerized knowledge of the miraculous had done to the limitless imagination of the float makers. This year these creative geniuses had definitely outdone themselves.

I mention this to exonerate myself for my neglect and delay in getting around to winding Seth. For it was not until somewhere between the Cal Tech float and the British Columbia entry that the passing of time struck me, struck me with such force that I already visualized Old Seth breathing his last and thoroughly bereft due to my unforgiveable procrastination.

Pulling myself away from the passing parade, I hurried into my study where Seth stood with his back against the wall. Even before I reached him and before I would ordinarily have noticed, I was assured by the swinging pendulum that he was still alive and well.

In my anxiety to lay hands on the winding key which normally should have been in its accustomed place behind the right-hand corner of the rosewood case, I realized that I had misplaced it (also for the first time in my life), and when I finally located it behind the left-hand corner and snapped it up, I said, aloud, "Sorry I'm late, Seth!"

It was then that my fantasy began, for above his ticking and my winding of the gears, I would have sworn I heard him say, "Later than you think!" By the chuckle in his voice, you would never have guessed how late it must have been for him. The only clue that gave him away was that he was going on nine and was preparing to strike. It was then that his voice faltered and, as I turned the key carefully in the striking arbor, he experienced a few unsteady moments, but took it all in stride.

When the best I could come up with was, "Forgive me," he shot back with, "You may think you were late, but don't forget things are always in perfect time."

This was his was of reiterating what he had told me in previous conversations, the deployment of the belief that the direction of events is in more powerful hands than the hands of a clock, or any timepiece, for that matter. He once confided to me that this was the creed imparted to him by the clockmaster who fashioned him and who advised him to make the creed of "divine order" his code for life.

I should mention at this point that we had often got into conversations beyond our depths and certainly greater than my capacity to figure out. Fantasies now and then were taken for granted, as if they were part of the reality of life. For example, one evening during the Christmas season Seth and I were alone in the house, and I heard him strike the ten o'clock hour. I looked up from the my desk and got to thinking that his hands of a clock were a manifestation of the hands of TIME, which no one has ever seen anymore than anyone had ever seen the hands that moved the Bethlehem Star.

"Time itself," Seth said, as if reading my thoughts, "is largely in the mind of the observer." While he felt his time was constant, others might complain that it was too slow or too fast, according to their state of mind. Too fast for lovers, too slow for those in conflict, all too rapid for one's youth, too slow for the aged, and so on.

Seth and I then speculated on these things at length, trying to get a handle on something besides mere belief. What lay behind the symbols and the signs or beyond the images we live by? What was the magic and miracle that produced the phenomenon of Christmas? We rarely went so far as to bring God into our imagined conversations, but I remember how intrigued Seth was when I told him about my father's belief in the Creator as "the great I AM." Dad had a way of dismissing imponderables with a quip. *"How long did it take I AM to make the world?"* he once asked challengingly, then answered his own question. *"No time at all. He made the world before He ever made time."*

Seth liked this because he had a genuine affection for my dad on many counts. The great unseen, omnipotent, omniscient "I AM" was okay with Seth if one insisted on an answer to the question of a first cause from which all effects emanate and which at the same time allow that I AM might also be an identification for ourselves.

But on this midnight hour, as an afterthought to the reiteration of his creed and code, Seth suggested it might be well for us to give a thought not only to Christmas, but to the New Year as well. "Let's make a resolution," he said. "I resolve to keep on keeping time if you'll resolve not to let time keep you."

"Tick that past me again," I told him.

"Gladly," he replied with a laugh. "The point is, I always have time on my hands. That is part of my job. But when you have time on your hands, you have time on your mind and make a big thing out of it. Especially at Christmas. You keep hanging around as though you were running out of time."

"Okay," I countered because of an inner feeling that our precious relationship might have been jeopardized a bit by my delayed attention to his needs during this season, although my feeling may have been entirely a self-engendered sense of guilt. At any rate, I was anxious to patch things up, so I said, "As to whether we can keep the resolution, only time will tell!"

Seth picked this up instantly. "There you go," he said, "using phrases which even I, in my position, hesitate to use. Have you ever heard me say: *Time will tell? I'll be with you in a minute? Give me just five minutes? I've wasted a whole hour? I am pressed for time? Where did the day go? It was a long night? It was a short night? Time flies? Here comes another Christmas? Time passes, we stay? We pass on, time stays?* Wouldn't you say these expressions are rather *time-*

worn, especially between you and me? Shouldn't we sometime take time to get at the heart of things rather than to talk all around them?"

During this interplay when he was ticking off the cliches I had used through the years, we were looking at each other face to face as if for the first time. I could not remember that his voice had ever been so hushed as when he closed his recapitulation. Although fearful I might break the spell with just another time-tempered phrase, I found myself saying it. "By the way, Seth, have I told you lately that I loved you?"

"I was about to ask the very same question!" he said, turning the tables on me, for truth was, I hadn't spoken of love at any time through the busy holiday season. "Yes," he repeated, "I was going to talk about love, too, but I didn't think it was necessary, not between us."

"Exactly!" I chimed in. "Not between us!" and, with this, I laid the winding key carefully in its proper place while the free and easy swing of the pendulum worked its old-time magic.

"Tell me, Seth," I said with new enthusiasm, "how many hours would you say that you and I have dialogued together through the years, and through how many ticks of your heart and mind have we been together?"

"Heavens," said Seth, "that's something only TIME can tell!"

It was not only what he said, but the way he said it that got the truth through to me that we had more in common than I ever cared to admit. In all our years we had talked all around the subject of TIME, but never had we explored the personification or the true relationship of TIME and life and love.

Never throughout our relationship had we ever fully expressed what we felt, as if fearful of the mysteries involved, the hidden nature of the unknown, the speculation of something too fatalistic, too far beyond the reach of us.

It was only now at *Christmastime* that we saw each other in the knowledge that, after all, he was only a timepiece and not the Time Keeper, and I was only his key person and not the actual Keeper of the Key. Because of Christmas, both of us were willing to admit that we were ruled by a power higher and greater than ourselves.

"Tell me, Seth," I whispered, "have you ever seen him?"

"TIME?"

"Yes, Father TIME."

"Oh, come now," he chided with a laugh.

"Well, Father-Mother TIME, or whatever!" I retorted.

"Never have I seen TIME," Seth confessed. "Though I have manifested TIME and made believe I knew a great deal about TIME, and even though I have often felt TIME creeping up on me....Forgive me! Time *creeping up on me* is the most abominable and overused of all time's phrases!"

As he wound this up with a self-accusing laugh, Old Seth appeared younger and freer than I had ever known him to be. His hands, moving at ten-forty, seemed to be covering one of his eyes, holding back more humor than he cared to show. The arbor winding gears were for all the world like dimples in his cheeks, the Roman numerals could have been a wreath of flowers, and the swinging pendulum a designer's symbol of perpetual motion.

"My dear Seth," I exlaimed, "you have finally put everything into perspective. My assumption that whenever I am speaking to you, I am conversing directly with TIME may have been an illusion, but it may in fact be the nearest to the source that we are ever permitted to venture. Let's live by what we know, and let the unknown take care of itself. When *it* wants us to know and feels we have the right to know and the capacity to know what we need to know, well and good. Let it all be in TIME. Right?"

"Right!" he agreed, his hands moving steadily.

"You have helped me immeasurably," I assured him. "Whenever I come to you with my thoughts or troubles, you always have time for me. So even though we don't know where TIME is or where TIME comes from or where it is going, or if it even exists at all, for me to speak of TIME apart from you is like speaking of the Creator apart from His or Her creation. In short, Seth, as you once suggested, Whoever made us gave us the tick of life. But because this one and only Creator can be known only by way of created things, let's raise a toast to ourselves and Christmastime!"

"To ourselves and Christmastime!" chimed Seth, and as I agreed and lifted an imaginary glass of holiday cheer, I heard a voice. Soundless as silence and clear as a bell, it came, I promise you, from inside the rosewood case. With a ring of exuberance it said, "I'll drink to that!"

"It's TIME!" said Seth, striking the 11th hour.

Before I could get myself organized, it was as if our dialogue was starting all over again on a revolving screen spinning off sequences of unfolding years, and out of a kaleidoscope of sights and sounds, TIME was waving his hands and saying, "I was just passing by!"

I was grateful that Seth was sufficiently wound up and in control to bombard TIME with what was a shouted question at the passing scene, "Hey! Who *is* the Keeper and the Winder of the Key?"

And TIME rewarded us by calling back over his shoulder, "I AM!"

Seth, having finished striking the hour, sighed and whispered to himself, "He's always been elusive."

With this he turned to me and said, "Go back to your Christmas duties and let me think!"